PROVENCE *EASY*

United Kingdom
Belgium
Germany
Luxembourg
St-Malo
Paris
Strasbourg
FRANCE
Switzerland
Atlantic Ocean
Bordeaux
Lyon
Italy
Provence
Avignon
Riviera
Nice
Toulouse
Marseille
Spain
Andorra
Mediterranean Sea

Andy Herbach

Made Easy
Travel Guides

Made Easy
Travel Guides

www.madeeasytravelguides.com

PROVENCE MADE EASY
Fifth edition
ISBN: 9798391681243
Text and Maps Copyright © 2023 by Andy Herbach
- All Rights Reserved -

Acknowledgments
Contributor: Karl Raaum
All photos from Shutterstock, Pixabay, and Karl Raaum
Editor: Marian Modesta Olson

ABOUT THE AUTHOR

Andy Herbach is the author of the *Eating & Drinking* series of menu translators and restaurant guides, including *Eating & Drinking in Paris, Eating & Drinking in Italy, Eating & Drinking in Spain and Portugal, Eating & Drinking in Germany,* and *Eating & Drinking in Latin America*. He is also the author of several travel guides, including *Wining & Dining in Paris, Wining & Dining in Italy, The Amazing California Desert, Palm Springs Made Easy, Southern California Made Easy, Paris Walks, The Next Time I See Paris, Europe Made Easy, Paris Made Easy, Amsterdam Made Easy, Berlin Made Easy, Barcelona Made Easy, Madrid Made Easy, Oslo Made Easy, Nice and the French Riviera Made Easy, Provence Made Easy,* and *Wales Made Easy*. Andy is a lawyer and resides in Palm Springs, California.

You can e-mail corrections, additions, and comments to eatndrink@aol.com or through www.madeeasytravelguides.com.

TABLE OF CONTENTS

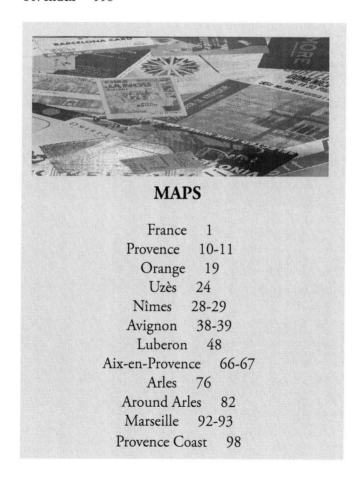

MAPS

Reviews for travel guides by Andy Herbach
•

"...an opinionated little compendium."
Eating & Drinking in Paris
~ New York Times

"Everything you need to devour Paris on the quick."
Best of Paris
~ Chicago Tribune

"an elegant, small guide..."
Eating & Drinking in Italy
~ Minneapolis Star Tribune

"Makes dining easy and enjoyable."
Eating & Drinking in Spain
~ Toronto Sun

"Guide illuminates the City of Light."
Wining & Dining in Paris
~ Newsday

"This handy pocket guide is all you need..."
Paris Made Easy
~ France Magazine

"Small enough for discreet use..."
Eating & Drinking in Paris
~ USA Today

"It's written as if a friend were talking to you."
Eating & Drinking in Italy
~ Celebrity Chef Tyler Florence

1. INTRODUCTION

Some come for the savory cuisine and wonderful wines, while others visit quiet villages to get away from it all. There are also some of the world's best-preserved Roman ruins to see, and elegant seaside resorts where you can bask on sun-drenched beaches. Whatever your reasons to visit, there's truly something for everyone in Provence.

You'll be dazzled by fields of lavender, yellow sunflowers, and bright red poppies under brilliant blue skies. Wherever you go, you'll create colorful memories.

You'll have over 100 places of interest at your fingertips (from the Papal Palace in Avignon to the wineries in Châteauneuf-du-Pape to the beaches in Cassis), with insider tips on cafes, restaurants, hotels, shops, outdoor markets, and where to sample Provence's great wines. We'll visit the loveliest towns of Provence, including Aix-en-Provence, Arles, Avignon, and Nîmes.

This guide covers all the information you need to plan your trip without burdening you with a long list of options that simply aren't worth your precious vacation time. Forget those bulky travel books. This handy little guide is all you need to make your visit enjoyable, memorable–and *easy*!

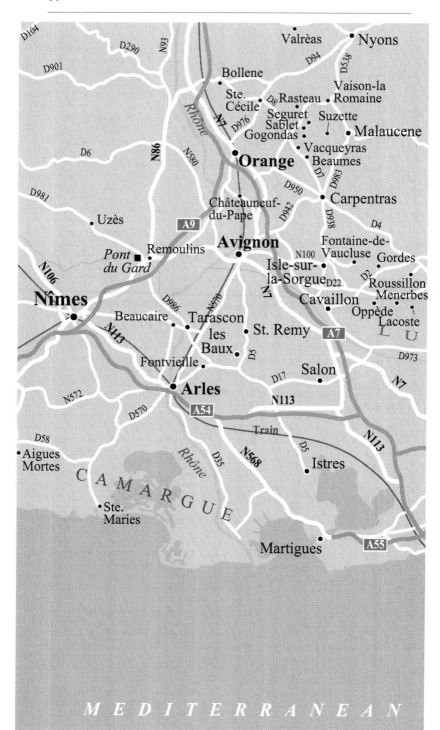

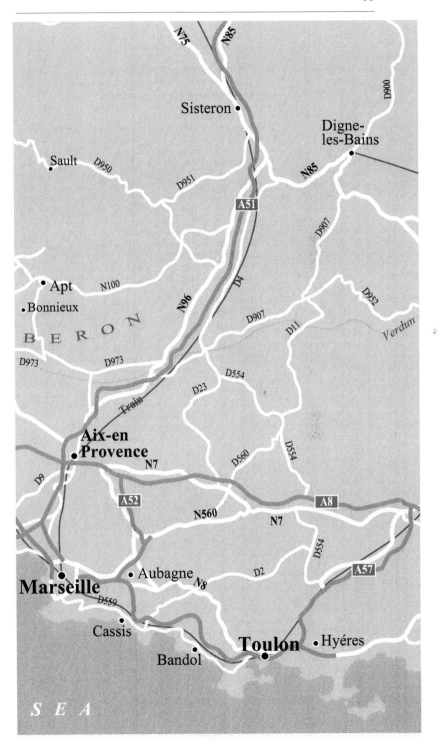

2. OVERVIEW

Get ready to explore Roman ruins, eat fantastic food, enjoy bustling outdoor markets, or just sit in the sun and sip a glass of chilled wine.

The Main Cities of Provence

Arles is one of the three "A's" that make up the most visited cities in Provence (along with Aix-en-Provence and Avignon). Arles has everything you could want in a Provence city: festivals, an Old Town, Roman ruins, cafes, and intimate restaurants.

Aix-en-Provence is a graceful and sophisticated city. Between the 12th and 15th centuries it was the capital of Provence. Shaded squares with bubbling fountains in the Old Quarter, 17th-century town houses, and the cours Mirabeau (the grand main avenue) make Aix a must for all visitors to Provence.

Although the last pope left in 1377, you're reminded of the papal legacy everywhere in modern-day **Avignon**. Its large student population makes it a vibrant city unlike most of the small villages of Provence.

Officially part of the Languedoc region, **Nîmes** is a popular destination for visitors to Provence. Some of the world's best-preserved Roman sights are here, giving it the nickname "the Rome of France."

Marseille is France's oldest city. Many travelers, put off by its urban sprawl, avoid it, as most come to this part of the country for quiet villages. Those who do choose to spend time here will be rewarded, as Marseille is a vibrant and cosmopolitan city.

LOVELY VILLAGES OF PROVENCE

There are so many lovely villages in Provence that it's hard to pick favorites. Depending on your interest, here are a few of our favorites:

Saignon: Quiet and Unspoiled
Lourmarin: Fine Dining
Oppède-de-Vieux: A Taste of Old Provence
L'Isle-sur-la-Sorge: The "Venice of Provence"
Uzès: An Overlooked Gem
Cassis: Sun-Drenched Beaches
St-Rémy-de-Provence: Calm and Sophisticated
Les Baux-de-Provence: Dramatic and Majestic
Roussillon: Incredibly Colorful

3. NORTHERN PROVENCE

HIGHLIGHTS
- Roman ruins, especially those at Nîmes and the Pont du Gard
  - Unspoiled medieval villages like Séguret
  - Beautiful wine country, centered around Châteauneuf-du-Pape
  - Undiscovered gems like the village of Uzès

Northern Provence is home to impressive Roman structures like the **Pont du Gard**, the ruins found in the fortified medieval village of **Vaison-la-Romaine**, the massive theatre of **Orange**, and some of the world's best-preserved Roman sights of **Nîmes**, "the Rome of France." After you've viewed the extraordinary Roman sights, you can slow down in the quaint villages of **Séguret** and **Le Barroux** or head to undiscovered **Uzès**. Top it all off by drinking the delicious wines of the vineyards of **Châteauneuf-du-Pape.**

Northern Provence is in the south of France. The largest city, Nîmes, has a population of 150,000. The towns are within 25 miles (40 km) of Avignon and about 400 miles (644 km) south of Paris.

Vaison-la-Romaine
The fortified medieval village of **Vaison-la-Romaine** seems to hang precariously over the road as you approach. It's 20 miles (32 km) northeast of Avignon/17 miles (27 km) northeast of Orange. Vaison-la-Romaine can be reached from Avignon by bus (90 minutes) and Orange by bus (45 minutes).

The village is divided into two by the Ouvèze River. The Roman bridge connects **Ville-Basse** (the Roman and present-day town) and **Ville-Haute** (the medieval town). A lively market fills place François-Cevert every Tuesday morning and early afternoon.

Head to the Roman Ruins in the Ville-Basse. The ruins are split by a modern road (avenue Général-de-Gaulle). The **Quartier de Puyim** has remains of a 6,000-seat theatre, temples, courthouse (praetorium), and foundations of homes including the **Maison des Messii**. The **Musée Théo-Desplans**, an archeology museum, is here. Across the street is the **Quartier de la Villasse** with the remains of a Roman village, including its baths (and marble toilets). *Info: In Ville Basse (Avenue Général-de-Gaulle). Tel. 04/90.46.51.14. Open daily Apr-Sep 9:30am-6pm, Feb, Nov, and Dec 10am-noon and 2pm-5pm, Mar and Oct 10am-12:30pm and 2pm-5:30pm. Closed Jan. Admission: €9, under 9 free (includes admission to the cathedral see next page). www.provenceromaine.com.*

Also worth a look is the **Cathédral Notre-Dame-de-Nazareth.** One of the finest examples of Provençal Romanesque architecture, this cathedral is known for its sculpted cloister. *Info: Avenue Jules-Ferry. Open daily10am-5pm (until 6pm in summer). Closed Jan. Admission: €9, under 9 free (includes admission to the archeology museum, see prior page). www.provenceromaine.com.*

Now it's time to head to the **Haute Ville** (Upper Town). From the Roman ruins on avenue Général-de-Gaulle toward the river, you'll cross the 2,000-year-old Roman bridge (**Pont Romain**). In the 1990s, a flood destroyed a nearby modern bridge, but left the Roman bridge intact! Explore the fortified medieval village high above the river valley. You'll pass 13th- and 14th-century homes on your way through a twisted maze of steep cobblestone streets. At the highest point are the ruins of a castle built in 1160 by the Count of Toulouse.

While in the Upper Town, you're going to get quite hungry climbing the steep streets. A good place to relax, eat, and drink is on the garden terrace of **La Fontaine** at the Beffroi Hotel (*see below*).

Vaison-la-Romaine Sleeping & Eating
Hôtel Beffroi €-€€
Located in a beautiful 16th-century mansion in the Upper Town, this 22-room, family-owned hotel offers panoramic views of the surrounding area. There's a garden terrace, an outdoor pool, and parking both at the hotel (a rarity in the Upper Town) and at the foot of the Upper Town. *Info: Rue de l'Évêché (in the Upper Town). Tel. 04/90.36.04.71. V, MC, AE. TV, telephone, hairdryer. minibar. Restaurant (€€). Open May-Oct for dinner Fri-Sun. No lunch Mon and Thu. www.le-beffroi.com.*

Séguret & Le Barroux

We'll visit two medieval villages today: Séguret and Le Barroux.

The quaint medieval village of **Séguret** clings to the foothills of the **Dentelles de Montmirail**, a series of limestone rocks stretching skyward. It's five miles (nine km) southwest of Vaison-la-Romaine. You can climb its car-free and steep cobblestone streets lined with vine-covered stone homes. There are three medieval gateways, the 12th-century church **Eglise St-Denis**, a 15th-century fountain, and castle ruins. A truly lovely town. Take in the sweeping views of the vineyards on the plain below and don't leave this area without stopping at one (or a few) of them.

We recommend you unwind at **Le Mesclun** (€€-€€€), a village restaurant serving Provençal dishes. Splendid views of the surrounding vineyards from the outdoor terrace. *Info: 208 rue des Poternes. Tel. 04/90.46.93.43. Closed Sun dinner, Tue dinner, and Wed. Open Jul and Aug Thu-Tue, closed Wed. Cooking classes also provided from €110. www.lemesclun.com.*

If you thought Séguret was unspoiled, wait until you see **Le Barroux**! It's ten miles (16 km) south of Vaison-la-Romaine/21 miles (34 km) northeast of Avignon. A maze of narrow streets with ancient fountains makes this unspoiled hill town worth a visit. You can tour the restored vaulted rooms of the imposing fortified *château* and Renaissance chapel. The castle is a frequent site for contemporary art exhibits. *Info: Tel. 06/59.13.13.21. Open daily May-Sep 10:30am-6:45pm, Oct-Apr 10:30am-1pm and 2pm-5:45pm. Admission: €5. www.chateaudubarroux.fr.*

Le Barroux Sleeps and Eats

Les Géraniums €

This family-owned, 22-room hotel in an unspoiled hill town also has a lovely restaurant. Relax on the beautiful flowered terrace where meals are served. Try the *plateau de fromages de France*, a platter of delicious French cheeses. *Info: Place de la Croix. Tel. 04/90.62.41.08. V, MC. Restaurant (€€-€€€). Open daily. www.hotel-geraniums-lebarroux.com.*

Orange

Today we'll visit the magnificent Roman structures of Orange. It's 19 miles (31 km) north of Avignon/six miles (10 km) north of Châteauneuf-du-Pape.

Orange's name dates back to when it was governed by the Dutch House of Orange. It became a thriving Roman city filled with public baths, temples, and monuments. In the 13th century, many of the Roman buildings were demolished and the stone used to build a defensive wall. Today most visitors come to this town overlooking the Rhône Valley to see two magnificent Roman structures that survived.

The massive Roman theatre (**Théâtre Antique**) was built in the time of Caesar Augustus, and his statue on the center stage still survives. This is the best-preserved Roman theatre in the world. Its acoustic wall remains, and if you climb the stairs to the top of the semi-circle of theatre seats you can still hear conversations of those on the stage: a testament to the acoustical-engineering skills of its classical designers. Plays and musical events are still held here, and there's an opera and classical music fair, called Les Chorégies d'Orange, every July. (*www.choregies.fr*). An archeological dig of an ancient gymnasium is located adjacent to the theatre. Also on the same square is the **Musée d'Orange**. This small museum displays Roman antiquities and has a gift shop. It's across the street from the Théâtre Antique.

Info: Place des Frères-Mounet/Rue Madeleine Roch. Tel. 04/90.51.17.60. Open Jan, Feb, Nov, and Dec 9:30am-4:30pm; Mar and Oct 9:30am-5:30pm; Apr, May, and Sep 9am-6pm; Jun-Aug 9am-7pm. Admission: €10 (includes audio guide and entry to the Théâtre Antique), under 7 free. www.theatre-antique.com.

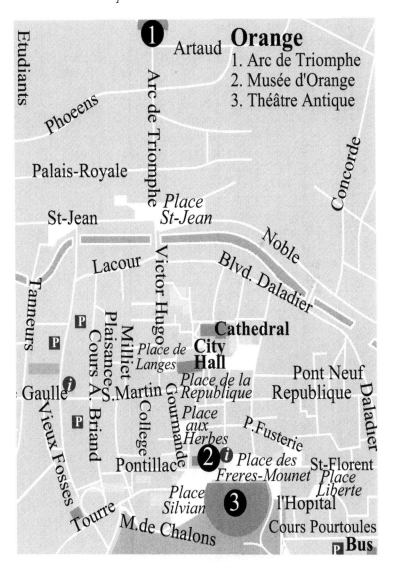

Orange
1. Arc de Triomphe
2. Musée d'Orange
3. Théâtre Antique

If you're really into Roman structures, check out the **Arc de Triomphe** north of the city center at the traffic circle on avenue Arc de Triomphe (in the direction of Gap). This incredibly well-preserved 60-foot-tall Roman arch was built around 27 BC, and is decorated with battle scenes of the Gallic War.

Orange Sleeping & Eating

Le Grand Hôtel d'Orange €€
Four town houses have been combined to create this unique 40-room hotel in the historic Old Town. Traditional furnishings, a helpful staff, and a quiet location on a pedestrian street all make this a good option while in Orange. Some rooms have been recently renovated. *Info: Place de Langes. Tel. 04/90.11.40.40. V, MC, AE. TV, telephone, minibar, hairdryer, safe, pool, fitness room.* Modern French cuisine is served at the hotel's **Le Garden**. *Tel. 04/90.11.40.40. Closed Mon and Tue. €€-€€€. www.grandhotelorange.com.*

Hôtel Le Glacier €-€€
This family-run hotel has a fine location just a few blocks from the Roman Theater. Rooms vary in size, but all are clean and nicely decorated. There's also secure parking. Good choice if you want to walk to all the sights. Friendly welcome. *Info: 46 Cours Aristide Briand. Tel. 04/90.34.02.01. V, MC. AC, TV.* **Bistrot Le Glacier** (€€) serves local fare, burgers, and wine from small local producers. *www.le-glacier.com.*

La Grotte d'Auguste €€ €€€
The name of this restaurant means "Auguste's Cave." This unique restaurant, located inside the Théâtre Antique, serves Provençal fare in stone rooms (a cave). In the summer, you can sit on the terrace and enjoy a splendid view of the massive Roman theatre. *Info: Théâtre Antique/Rue Madeleine Roch. Tel. 04/90.60.22.54. Closed Sun and Mon. www.restaurant-orange.fr.*

Orange Shopping/Market

Thursday-morning food, local crafts, and flea market on cours A.-Briand. 300 vendors are spread out on place Georges Clemenceau and place André Bruey.

WINE TASTING
You're in the heart of wine country. Look for signs saying *Cave Coopérative* at vineyards. If they say *dégustation*, this means free wine tastings are offered. Although there's no obligation to buy, you should get at least one bottle (especially if you've spent some time at the winery).

Châteauneuf-du-Pape
Get ready to drink some wine in **Châteauneuf-du-Pape**. It's six miles (10 km) south of Orange/14 miles (23 km) west of Carpentras/11 miles (18 km) north of Avignon.

This town's history is linked to the popes of Avignon. The *château* towering over the town was built by the popes in the 14th century as a summer residence, and was badly damaged by bombing during World War II. Vineyards, said to have been planted by the popes, surround the lovingly restored town whose names means "new castle of the pope." Today, the wines from this area are known the world over. In 1954 the village council passed an ordinance prohibiting the landing of flying saucers (they called them "flying cigars") in their vineyards. (This ordinance has worked well in discouraging such landings).

A wine festival (**Fête de la Véraison**) is held for three days in early August. Locals dress in medieval costumes, and area wineries set up stalls. For about €5, you purchase a souvenir glass and sample all the wine you want. If you start seeing wine coming out of the attractive fountain in the place du Portail, you're not that drunk; it really does spurt wine during the festival.

After exploring the town, head to route D17, and stop at the **Musée du Vin/Caves Brotte**. Located in the cellar (*cave*) of a family winery, this museum celebrates the area's wine making tradition. And yes, there are wine tastings. *Info: Avenue le Bienheureux Pierre du Luxembourg (route D17). Tel. 04/90.83.59.44. Open daily 9am-11:45am and 2pm-5:45pm. Admission: €8 (includes tasting of three wines). www.museeduvinbrotte.com.*

There are over 20 area wineries where you can taste the wines of **Châteauneuf-du-Pape. Clos des Papes** is conveniently located on the route to Avignon. *Info: 13 avenue le Bienheureux Pierre du Luxembourg (route D17). Tel. 04/90.83.70.13. Open daily.*

Châteauneuf-du-Pape Sleeping & Eating

Le Restaurant du Verger des Papes €€-€€€
Impressive views from this attractive restaurant located on a hill overlooking the city. You can visit the *cave* and choose a bottle of wine for dinner. Start your meal with *foie gras* and have the specialty, roasted lamb (*agneau*). You may want to try one of the dishes featuring *pistou* (a sauce made of garlic, basil, nuts, and olive oil), the Provençal version of Italian pesto. *Info: 2 rue Château. Tel. 04/90.83.50.40. Closed Sun and Mon. vergerdespapes.com.*

La Maisouneta €€-€€€
This friendly and comfortable restaurant serves Provençal specialties. It's conveniently located in the center of this attractive town. The house specialty is *magret de canard* (duck breast). Try the grilled version with honey and lavender. Good choice of *pâtes fraiches* (fresh pasta dishes). A selection of local wines is available and there are occasional wine tastings. *Info: Place Jean Moulin at rue de République. Tel. 04/90.32.55.03. Closed Sun and Mon. www.la-maisouneta.fr.*

Château des Fines Roches €€-€€€
This 11-room hotel is quite unique. It's located in a former *château*. The 19th-century building has been renovated and has been a hotel since the 1970s. It's conveniently located outside of Châteaunuef-du-Pape and only six miles (10 km) from Avignon. Fabulous swimming pool and beautiful views of the surrounding vineyards. *Info: 1901 Route de Sorgues. Tel. 04/90.83.70.23. Closed Jan. www.chateaufinesroches.com.*

The gourmet restaurant here **La Table des Fines Roches** (€€€) serves innovative French and Provençal cuisine. The restaurant's terrace is a lovely place to dine. The *cave* (wine cellar) is known for its selection of wines from Châteaunuef-du-Pape. A wonderful choice to dine at lunch. Fixed-price menus from €34. *Closed Mon, Tue, and Sun dinner.*

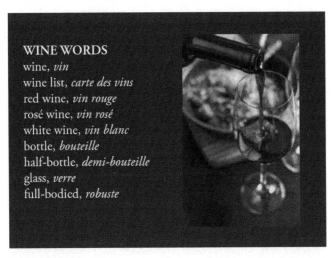

WINE WORDS
wine, *vin*
wine list, *carte des vins*
red wine, *vin rouge*
rosé wine, *vin rosé*
white wine, *vin blanc*
bottle, *bouteille*
half-bottle, *demi-bouteille*
glass, *verre*
full-bodied, *robuste*

Pont du Gard

Today we'll view Roman ingenuity at the Pont du Gard (*see photo on page 14*). It's 23 miles (37 km) southwest of Orange/13 miles (22 km) southwest of Avignon. Pont du Gard can be reached from Avignon by bus (50 minutes). *See cover photo.*

How did they do it? Two thousand years ago, the Romans built a system to carry water 30 miles from a spring near Uzès to Nîmes. The Pont du Gard is a huge three-tiered, arched aqueduct spanning the Gardon River. It's the second tallest Roman structure in the world. Only the Coliseum in Rome is taller.

The aqueduct once carried 44 million gallons each day. The 80-foot main arch is the largest ever built by the Romans. When we first visited the aqueduct, you were able to walk on the very top (a scary and dangerous experience).

Today, the aqueduct is off-limits. Visitors flock here and marvel at the sheer size of this tribute to Roman ingenuity. A museum at the visitor center highlights the history of the aqueduct, and there's an informative film that plays every half hour. Ludo is an interactive kids' zone (in English). There's a cafe for light meals and a restaurant offering regional specialties. You can swim in the river below, dive off part of the aqueduct, or rent a canoe

(which is a great way to experience the aqueduct). *Info: Tel.
04/66.37.50.99. Open daily Nov-Feb 9am-5pm, Mar and Oct
9am-6pm, Apr-June and Sep 9am-7pm, Jul and Aug 9am-8pm.
Admission: €6.50, under 18 free. Parking is €9.
www.pontdugard.fr.*

Uzès

Don't bypass **Uzès** on the border of Provence in the Languedoc
region. It's 15 miles (25 km) north of Nîmes/24 miles (39 km)
west of Avignon. Uzès can be reached from Avignon by bus (80
minutes).

Begin your visit to this lovely town at the imposing **Cathédrale
St-Théodorit** (you can't miss it, and there's a large car park next
to it). The cathedral, built on the site of a Roman temple, dates
back to 1652. Those are the remains of St-Firmin in the glass
coffin on the left side of the cathedral.

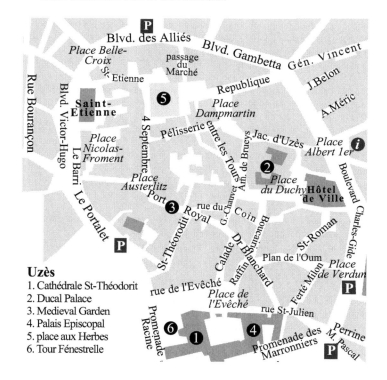

Uzès
1. Cathédrale St-Théodorit
2. Ducal Palace
3. Medieval Garden
4. Palais Episcopal
5. place aux Herbes
6. Tour Fénestrelle

Organ concerts are held in the Cathédrale St-Théodorit, especially the last two weeks of July, during the musical festival **Nuits Musicales d'Uzès**. The concerts are played on its 2,700-pipe organ which has been in use since the 17th century. *www.nuitsmusicalesuzes.org.*

When outside, look up at the **Tour Fénestrelle**. Doesn't it look like the Leaning Tower of Pisa? As you face the cathedral, there's a former palace to your left (Palais Episcopal) that now houses the city's courts of law.

Across the street from the cathedral is the Old Town where you'll find the ducal palace on place du Duché. Descendents of the House of Uzès still live here.

Take a walk around the beautiful and car-free Old Town, and visit the **medieval garden** on rue Port Royal. *Info: Tel. 04/66.22.38.21. Open daily Jul and Aug 10am-1pm and 2pm-6pm, Apr-Jun and Sep 2pm-6pm, Oct-Nov 2pm-5:30pm. Admission: €7. www.jardinmedievaluzes.com.*

The **place aux Herbes,** with sheltered walkways and medieval homes, is a relaxing place to take a coffee break, although it's not so calm on Wednesday mornings and Saturdays when it hosts a lively market.

Uzès Sleeping & Eating
Hôtel Entraigues €€
This 21-room hotel is housed in a former 15th-century mansion near the cathedral. It has been completely renovated, with a lovely swimming pool and a good restaurant, serving food on the terrace. *Info: Place de l'Évêché. Tel. 04/66.72.05.25. V, MC, AE. Restaurant, bar, outdoor pool, AC, TV, telephone, minibar, hairdryer, safe. www.hotel-entraigues.com.*

La Table d'Uzès €€€

This award-winning restaurant will not disappoint. Dine indoors or outdoors in the attractive courtyard. Try the flavorful *filet mignon de porc*. The restaurant has a large selection of wines from the Languedoc region. Located in the lovely **La Maison d'Uzès Hotel (€€€)**. They often offer a spa and lunch combination. *Info: 18 rue Docteur Blanchard. Tel. 04/66.20.07.00. Open Wed-Sun. www.lamaisonduzes.fr.*

Nîmes

Officially part of the Languedoc region, **Nîmes** is a popular destination for visitors to Provence. It's 26 miles (43 km) southwest of Avignon/19 miles (31 km) northwest of Arles. Nîmes can be reached from Avignon by bus (90 minutes) and by train (40 minutes).

Some of the world's best-preserved Roman sights are here, giving it the nickname "the Rome of France." The town is dotted with Roman ruins. It's frenetic and not at all like the calm small villages of Provence. Did you know that denim (the material that all those jeans are made of) was created here in the Middle Ages? The Old Town is easily explored on foot, and is home to the major sights. Head to the tourist office at 6 boulevard des Arènes where you can pick up a free map. *Tel. 04/66.58.38.00. Open daily 9am-6pm (Apr-Oct until 7pm). www.nimes-tourisme.com.*

The steel-and-glass **Carré d'Art** is home to a contemporary art museum featuring works created after 1960. You can stop for refreshments at the rooftop cafe. It has a great view of the Roman temple and other landmarks. The museum is known for its collection of Arte Povera ("poor art"), a movement of artists who created sculpture through the use of humble, everyday materials. *Info: Place de la Maison Carrée. Tel. 04/66.76.35.70. Open Tue-Fri 10am-6pm, Sat and Sun 10am-6:30pm. Closed Mon. Admission: €8. www.carreartmusee.com.*

Head across the street. Built around 5 BC, the incredibly well-preserved **Maison Carrée** is a Roman temple modeled after the Temple of Apollo in Rome. It was the model for the Eglise de la Madeleine in Paris, the state capitol of Virginia, and many other buildings featuring Corinthian columns. The interior houses changing exhibits. *Info: Place de la Comédie (boulevard Victor-Hugo). www.arenes-nimes.com. See photo on page 31.*

As you leave the Roman temple, the street between it and the art museum is boulevard Victor Hugo. Head down the boulevard. You'll pass the place de la Madeleine (to your right on boulevard Victor Hugo). Soon you'll see a large arena.

Look familiar? The well-preserved arena (**Amphithéâtre Romain**) is a miniature of the Colosseum in Rome (*see photo below*). It held over 20,000 people who watched gladiators fight. Today, it's used for performances and an occasional bullfight. In the 13th century, the arena was inhabited by nearly 700 people who created a miniature village inside. Napoleon changed all that when he designated it a historic monument. *Info: Place de Arènes. Tel. 04/66.21.82.56. Open daily 9:30am-5pm (Jan, Feb, Nov, and Dec), 9am-6pm (Mar and Oct), 9am-6:30pm (Apr, May, and Sep), 9am-7pm (Jun), 9am-8pm (Jul and Aug). Admission: €10, under 7 free. A three-day pass for the arena, Maison Carrée, and Tour Magne is €13. www.arenes-nimes.com.*

Nîmes

1. Carré d'Art
2. Maison Carrée
3. Amphithéâtre Romain
4. Musée Archéologique et
   d'Histoire Naturelle
5. Porte d'Auguste
6. Eglise St-Baudile
7. Cathédral Notre-Dame et St-Castor
8. Musée du Vieux-Nîmes
9. Musée des Beaux-Arts
10. Jardin de la Fontaine
11. Musée de la Romanité

Across the street from the arena is the **Musée des Cultures Taurines**, a bullfighting museum, at 6 rue Alexandre-Ducros. *Info: Tel. 04/30.06.77.07. Open May-Oct Tue-Sun 10am-6pm. Closed Mon. Admission: €5. Currently closed.*

Also on the place de Arènes is the **Musée de la Romanité**. Roman history in Nîmes and the region is explored in this modern, fabulous museum with 65 multimedia displays. Great views from the rooftop (especially of the Arènes). There's also an archaeological garden. Don't miss this new edition to the city! *Info: 16 boulevard des Arènes. Tel. 04/48.21.02.20. Open Wed-Mon 10am-6pm (Apr-Oct until 7pm). Closed Tue. Admission: €9, under 7 free. www.museedelaromanite.fr.*

Other sights of interest here include the following on boulevard de l'Amiral-Courbet:

The **Musée Archéologique et d'Histoire Naturelle**, a museum of archaeology and natural history, is filled with statues, friezes, pottery, and coins. The ethnography and zoology rooms are especially popular with kids. Stuffed animals include Maurice, a giraffe from Niger, a Siberian Tiger, and a Canadian polar bear. *Info: 13 bis boulevard de l'Amiral-Courbet. Tel. 04/66.76.73.45. Open Tue-Sun 10am-6pm. Closed Mon. Admission: €5.*

The **Porte d'Auguste** is a gate built during the reign of Augustus. Across the street is the church **Eglise St-Baudile**, named after the martyr and patron saint of the city.

In the Old Town are two sights next to each other that are worth a visit.

The **Cathédral Notre-Dame et St-Castor** has a beautifully preserved Romanesque frieze featuring Adam, Eve, Abel, and Noah. Construction began on this cathedral in 1096. The inside features a 4th-century sarcophagus. *Info: Place aux Herbes. Open daily. Admission: Free.*

Off place aux Herbes (near the cathedral) is the **Musée du Vieux-Nîmes** (Museum of Old Nîmes) showcasing life in Nîmes in the Middles Ages, including a 14th-century jacket made of the famous denim de Nîmes, the fabric that Levi-Stauss used for blue jeans. *Info: Place aux Herbes. Tel. 04/66.76.70.56. Open Tue-Sun 10am-6pm. Closed Mon. Admission: €5. www.nimes.fr.*

The **Musée des Beaux-Arts** is the city's fine-arts museum. The museum is itself a work of art and is located in the former residence of a Ukrainian princess. You'll find not only French paintings and sculpture, but also a large collection of Flemish and Italian paintings, including Ruben's *Portrait of a Monk*. A well-preserved Gallo-Roman mosaic is also here as is Rodin's imposing sculpture *The Kiss. Info: Rue de la Cité-Foulc. Tel. 04/66.76.71.82. Open Tue-Sun 10am-6pm. Closed Mon. Admission: €5.*

One of the most beautiful gardens in all of France is the **Jardin de la Fontaine**. Designed in the 18th century, the chestnut trees shade statues, urns, and the remains of a Roman shrine. At the end of the garden are the ruins of the 1st-century **Temple de Diane**. Also here is the **Tour Magne** (a tower on Mont Cavalier and the city's oldest monument). *Info: End of quai de la Fontaine. Open daily. Admission: €3.50.*

Nîmes Sleeping and Eating

Maison Albar Hotel Nîmes Imperator €€€
This recently renovated 60-room hotel is located near one of the most beautiful gardens in all of France, the Jardin de la Fontaine. Rooms are decorated with traditional regional furnishings, and the bathrooms are quite modern. The lovely restaurant serves local specialties, and the bar opens onto the peaceful garden. *Info: Quai de la Fontaine. Tel. 04/66.21.90.30. V, MC, AE. Restaurant, bar, AC, TV, telephone, minibar, hairdryer, safe.* www.maison-albar-hotels-l-imperator.com.

Hôtel l'Amphithéâtre €
This 11-room hotel is the budget choice in Nîmes. Located in what were two private mansions from the 17th and 18th century, it's crammed with antiques. You may feel a little cramped in the small rooms (with small bathrooms), but the price and location are right. *Info: 4 rue des Arènes. Tel. 04/66.67.28.51. V, MC. TV, AC. Closed most of Jan.* www.hoteldelaamphitheatre.com.

Hôtel des Tuileries €-€€
Located near the Arènes and the train station, this hotel features 10 guest rooms and one suite. Comfortable rooms have small balconies. The owners are extremely helpful and friendly. Good value. *Info: 22 rue Roussy. Tel. 04/66.21.31.15. V, MC. TV, AC, hairdryer, refrigerator, safe, parking.* www.hoteldestuileries.com.

Skab €€€
This modern and elegant restaurant is located near the arena. Innovative Provençal cuisine and friendly service. Try the *pintade* (guinea hen) with *fleurs de courgettes* (zucchini flowers stuffed with cheese). Extensive wine list. *Info: 7 rue de la République. Tel. 04/66.21.94.30. Closed Sun, Mon, and part of Jan.* www.restaurant-skab.fr.

Le Ciel de Nîmes €€-€€€
This restaurant and cafe is located on the terrace atop the contemporary art museum Carré d'Art. Relax while you take in a great view of the city's sights. *Info: 16 place de la Maison Carrée. Tel. 04/66.36.71.70. Open 10am-6pm. Closed Mon. Open some evenings for dinner in summer.* www.lecieldenimes.fr.

There are lively cafes on boulevard Victor-Hugo and the area around the place de la Maison Carrée. You'll find plenty of cafes at the place de l'Horloge (Clock Square).

Nîmes Nightlife & Entertainment

Northern Provence is not known for its nightlife. Your best bet is in Nîmes.

For bars and nightlife, head to rue Fresque, rue Saint-Antoine, and rue de l'Etoile.

LGBTQ+

There are a few gay and gay-friendly establishments in Nîmes:
Lulu: *10 rue de la Curaterie. Tel. 04/66.36.28.20 (nightclub). www.lulu-club.com.*
Nîmes Sauna Club: *7-9 rue F. Pelloutier. Tel. 04/66.67.65.18 (sauna). www.nimesclubsauna.fr.*
Dancin': *8 bis rue Thoumayne. Tel. 04/26.03.17.30 (club). www.dancin.business.site.*

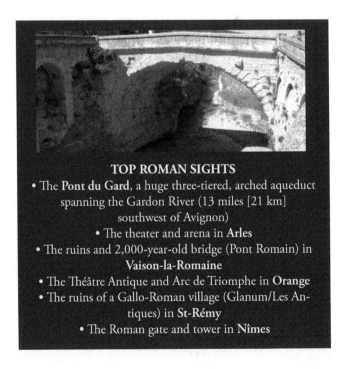

TOP ROMAN SIGHTS
- The **Pont du Gard**, a huge three-tiered, arched aqueduct spanning the Gardon River (13 miles [21 km] southwest of Avignon)
- The theater and arena in **Arles**
- The ruins and 2,000-year-old bridge (Pont Romain) in **Vaison-la-Romaine**
- The Théâtre Antique and Arc de Triomphe in **Orange**
- The ruins of a Gallo-Roman village (Glanum/Les Antiques) in **St-Rémy**
- The Roman gate and tower in **Nîmes**

4. AVIGNON

HIGHLIGHTS
- The place de l'Horloge, the heart of the city
- The colossal Papal Palace where seven popes ruled, and the Cathedral
- Musée Angladon, with art by Picasso, van Gogh, Degas, Cézanne...
- The famous bridge with its four arches
- Lovely bistros, cafes, restaurants, and hotels

In 1309, when Pope Clément V arrived after fleeing the corruption of Rome, the town became the capital of Christendom for 68 years. Although the last pope left in 1377, you're reminded of the papal legacy everywhere in modern day **Avignon**. Its large student population makes it a vibrant city, unlike most of the small villages of Provence. The students, upscale boutiques, and crowded cafes all make Avignon the most cosmopolitan city in Provence.

Avignon (population 92,000) is in the south of France. It's 60 miles (100 km) inland from the Mediterranean port city of Marseille, 51 miles (82 km) northeast of Aix-en-Provence, and 425 miles (685 km) south of Paris. Start your visit to Avignon by entering through the **Porte de la République**, one of the entries through the massive walls built by the Church. It's near the train station and parking lots. The tourist office is at 41 cours Jean-Jaurés. Tel. 04/32.74.32.74. Open daily 9am-6pm (Sun 10am-5pm). *www.avignon-tourisme.com.*

Avignon has a **TGV** (fast-speed train) station on the edge of town. The TGV station is connected to the Avignon Centre-Ville Station (in the central city) by TER, a local train. For more information on train travel to Avignon, see the *Planning Your Trip* section.

You can reach other destinations in Provence from Avignon by bus or train:
L'Isle-sur-la-Sorgue: 45 minutes by bus/30 minutes by train
Orange: 45 minutes by bus/15 minutes by train
Nîmes: 85 minutes by bus/40 minutes by train
Arles: 90 minutes by bus/20 minutes by train
St-Rémy-de-Provence: 60 minutes by bus
Pont du Gard: 65 minutes by bus
Le Baux: 65 minutes by bus
Uzès: 50 minutes by bus
Vaison-la-Romaine: 105 minutes by bus.

Sights

Musée Lapidaire

Located in a Jesuit chapel, this museum is filled with a collection of sculpture and stonework from the 1st and 2nd centuries. *Info: 27 rue de la République (at the corner of rue Frédéric Mistral). Tel. 04/90.85.75.38. Open Tue-Sun 10am-1pm and 2pm-6pm. Closed Mon. Admission: Permanent collection is free. www.musee-lapidaire.org.*

Musée Angladon

This museum houses the collection of Jacques Doucet, who established one the first fashion houses in Paris. It's filled with the works of Picasso, van Gogh, Degas, Modigliani, and Cézanne, to name a few. There's also a collection of furniture and art objects. *Info: 5 rue Laboureur (at the end of rue Frédéric Mistral). Tel. 04/90.82.29.03. Open Apr-Oct Tue-Sun 1pm-6pm. Closed Mon. Nov-Mar Tue-Sat 1pm-6pm, closed Mon and Sun. Admission: €8. www.angladon.com.*

Place de l'Horloge

This is the heart of the city, filled with bistros, cafes, and restaurants. It gets its name from the Gothic clock tower (**Tour du Jacquemart**). Great people-watching! On the square are the City Hall (**Hôtel de Ville**) and the 19th-century **Opéra House**. This square is a great place to take a break. Why don't you try a *pastis* (anise-flavored *aperitif*)? A Provençal word meaning mixture, it's a summer drink. Common brands are Pastis 51, Pernod, Ricard, Granier, Prado, and Henri Bardouin. *Info: On rue de la République. Just off the place de l'Horloge is the place du Palais (rue Phillipe connects the two squares).*

Papal Palace (Palais des Papes)

In 1309, French Pope Clément V was elected and moved to Avignon from Rome. For 68 years, popes ruled from here. In 1378, there were competing popes (one in Rome and one here). This schism continued until 1417. The popes in Avignon during this schism are referred to as the "antipopes." Benedict XII, the third pope to rule from Avignon, ordered the construction of this colossal palace that dominates Avignon. Today, you can tour the large palace. Be warned, it's mostly empty. The Great Court links the **Palais Vieux** (Old Palace) with the more decorated **Palais Nouveau** (New Palace). *See photo on page 34.*

Some highlights are:

- **Chapelle St-Jean**: with frescoes of the life of John the Baptist
- **Chapelle St-Martial**: with frescoes of the miracles of St. Martial
- **Banquet Hall** (Grand Tinel): with vaulted roof and 18th-century tapestries
- **Pope's Chamber**: the pontiff slept in this bedroom, whose blue walls are decorated with a vine-leaf motif
- **Council Hall** (Consistoire): with 14th-century frescoes
- **Chambre du Cerf**: featuring murals of a stag hunt and a decorated ceiling
- **Chapelle Clémentine**: where the college of cardinals met
- **Great Audience Hall** (Grande Audience): with frescoes of the prophets.

If you have time, stroll through the lovely Papal Gardens (€5, combined admission to gardens and palace is €14.50). *Info: Place du Palais. Tel. 04/90.27.50.00. Open daily Mar 1 to Nov 5 9am-9pm, Nov 6 to Dec 22 and Jan 1 to Feb 2 9am-6pm, Feb 3 to Feb 28 and Dec 23 to Dec 31 10am-6pm. Admission: €12 (including audio guide), under 8 free. www.palais-des-papes.com.*

Petit Palais

The former residence of cardinals and bishops is now the home of a museum devoted mostly to Italian paintings. Among them are works by Bellini, Botticelli, and Carpaccio. *Info: Place du Palais. Tel. 04/90.86.44.58. Open Wed-Mon 10am-1pm and 2pm-6pm. Closed Tue. Admission: Permanent collection is free. www.petit-palais.org. See photo below.*

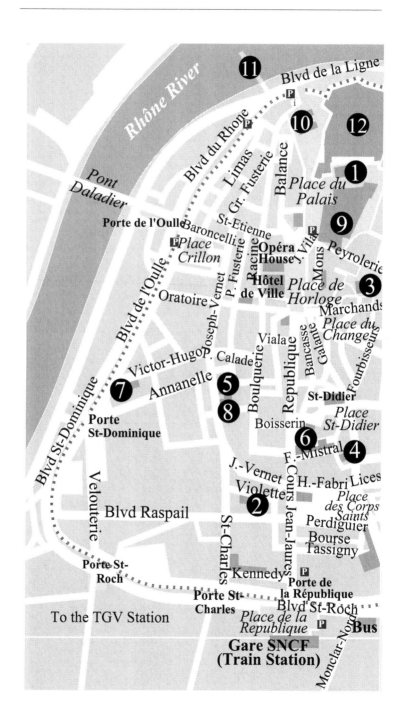

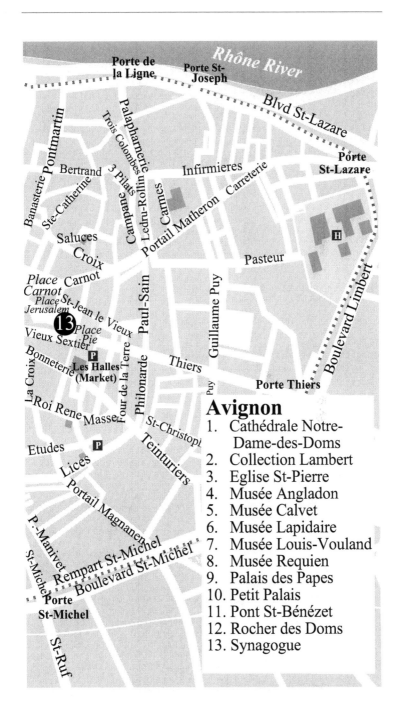

Avignon
1. Cathédrale Notre-
   Dame-des-Doms
2. Collection Lambert
3. Eglise St-Pierre
4. Musée Angladon
5. Musée Calvet
6. Musée Lapidaire
7. Musée Louis-Vouland
8. Musée Requien
9. Palais des Papes
10. Petit Palais
11. Pont St-Bénézet
12. Rocher des Doms
13. Synagogue

Cathédrale Notre-Dame-des-Doms

Some of the popes who ruled from the nearby Papal Palace are buried here in the Gothic tomb. The cathedral dates back to the 12th century. The gold statue of the Virgin that tops the cathedral is from the 19th century. *Info: Place du Palais. Tel. 04/90.82.12.21. Open Mon-Sat 6:30am-noon and 2:30pm-5:30pm (until 6pm in summer), Sun 9am-noon and 2:30pm-5:30pm. Admission: Free. www.cathedrale-avignon.fr.*

On the hill next to the cathedral is the **Rocher des Doms** (Rock of the Domes). You can enjoy the views across the Rhône River from this rocky bluff and garden. Huge pine trees, statues, and swans make this a lovely place to relax. There's a small vineyard down the slope. *Info: Montée du Moulin (on the hill next to the cathedral). Open daily. Admission: Free.*

Pont St-Bénézet (St. Bénézet Bridge)

There's a famous French children's song about this bridge: "Sur le pont d'Avignon on y danse, on y danse..." ("On the bridge of Avignon one dances, one dances..."). If that's the case, they better watch where they're stepping, as this arched bridge stretches across only part of the river. Legend has it that a shepherd named Bénézet was told by an angel to begin building the bridge in 1177. Only four arches of the original 22 remain, the rest having been destroyed by floods and war. There's a chapel on the bridge, and a small museum of the history of the bridge. *Info: Rue Ferruce. Tel. 04/32.74.32.74. Open daily. Admission: €5.*

Synagogue

Avignon's synagogue dates back to the 1200s. There's a memorial to Jews deported from here to the concentration camp at Auschwitz. *Info: 2 place Jérusalem. Tel. 04/90.85.21.24. Open Mon-Fri 10am-noon (hours vary). Closed Sat and Sun. Admission: Free.*

Eglise St-Pierre

You can admire the Gothic façade of a 12th-century church. The 16th-century carved doors depict the Annunciation, when the angel Gabrielle informed Mary that she would conceive a son. *Info: Place St-Pierre/Rue des Ciseaux d'Or. Open daily. Admission: Free.*

Musée Requien

This is one of the largest natural-history libraries in France. Most come to visit its herbarium which contains more than 200,000 specimens gathered by botanists from around the world. There's also an exhibit featuring the botany of Provence. *Info: 67 rue Joseph-Vernet. Tel. 04/90.82.43.51. Open Tue-Sat 10am-1pm and 2pm-6pm. Closed Sun and Mon. Admission: Free. www.museum-requien.org.*

Musée Calvet

Located in a beautiful 18th-century mansion, this museum (with a lovely garden) maintains a collection of antiquities (some of which are housed at the Musée Lapidaire above), and works by Manet, Brueghel, Corot, and David. *Info: 65 rue Joseph-Vernet. Tel. 04/90.86.33.84. Open Wed-Mon 10am-1pm and 2pm-6pm. Closed Tue. Admission: Permanent collection is free. www.musee-calvet.org.*

Musée Louis-Vouland

Located in a 19th-century mansion, this museum is filled with 17th- and 18th-century antiques, tapestries, and art objects. *Info: 17 rue Victor-Hugo. Tel. 04/90.86.03.79. Open Tue-Sun 2pm-6pm. Closed Mon and Jan. Admission: €6. www.vouland.com.*

Collection Lambert

The exterior of this 18th-century mansion doesn't look anything like the contemporary art inside. The museum houses the collection of Yvon Lambert, and includes more than 1,200 works of art dating from the 1960s to present. Interesting special exhibits. *Info: 5 rue Violette. Tel. 04/90.16.56.21. Open Wed-Sun 1pm-6pm. Closed Mon and Tue. Open daily Jul and Aug 11am-7pm. Admission: €10. www.collectionlambert.com.*

Villeneuve-lès-Avignon

If you want to get away from Avignon but don't want to drive, cross the bridge **Pont Daladier** over the Rhône River to Villeneuve-lès-Avignon (35-minute walk). Buses #122 and #123 depart from Avignon's Porte de l'Oulle stop. In the 1300s, cardinals built private estates here. The **Fort St-André** dominates the hilltop. The 13th-century **Tour Philippe le Bel** affords great views of Avignon and the Rhône Valley (*Tel. 04/32.70.08.57, Closed Mon and Jan. Admission: €4.50*). Also here are two sites on the rue de la République:

Musée Municipal Pierre-de-Luxembourg

The former residence of cardinals is now the home of a museum loaded with medieval sculpture and paintings. *Info: 3 rue de la République. Tel. 04/90.27.49.66. Closed Mon. Admission: €4.50.*

Chartreuse du Val-de-Bénédiction

Built in 1352, this is France's largest monastery. It was founded by Pope Innocent VI, who is buried here. You can visit the church, three cloisters, monastic cells, and splendid gardens. *Info: 58 rue de la République. Tel. 04/90.15.24.24. Open daily 9:30am-6:30pm (Oct to Mar 10am-5pm). Closed part of Jan. Admission: €8. You must book ahead at www.chartreuse.org.*

Avignon Sleeping & Eating
Hôtel de la Mirande €€€

This 20-room hotel, located in a 700-year-old town house behind the Papal Palace, is luxurious, comfortable, and elegant (with a renowned restaurant, too). Rooms are filled with antiques (num-

FESTIVAL D'AVIGNON
The **Festival d'Avignon**, an annual festival of dance, theater, and music is held most of July in Avignon. The squares are full of street performers, from good to absolutely awful. Can you say "mimes?" *www.festival-avignon.com.*

ber 20 is the most sought after). Truly an experience. *Info: 4 place de l'Amirande. Tel. 04/90.14.20.20. V, MC, AE. Restaurant, bar, TV, AC, telephone, minibar, hairdryer, safe. www.la-mirande.fr.*

Hôtel d'Europe €€€
A hotel since 1799 in a building dating back to the 1580s, this award-winning 44-room hotel is known for its central location, attentive service, and excellent restaurant, "La Vielle Fontaine." Its three suites have private terraces overlooking the Papal Palace. *Info: 14 place Crillon. Tel. 04/90.14.76.76. V, MC, AE. Restaurant, bar, TV, AC, telephone, minibar, hairdryer, safe. www.heurope.com.*

La Ferme €€-€€€
This 22-room hotel and restaurant are located about three miles (five km) from central Avignon in a 400-year-old farmhouse. Rooms and bathrooms are small. Great for those looking for a rustic and quiet place. The swimming pool is an added bonus. Parking is included. *Info: 110 Chemin des Bois - Île de la Barthelasse. Tel. 04/90.82.57.53. V, MC. AC, TV, telephone, hairdryer, parking. Dinner served daily, lunch on Sat and Sun. www.hotel-laferme.com.*

Mercure Pont d'Avignon €€
This hotel, part of a chain (with hotels in Marseille, Aix, and Nice), has 87 rooms, all with small bathrooms. Its central location can't be beat as it's near the foot of the Papal Palace. *Info: rue Ferruce. Tel. 04/90.80.93.93. V, MC, AE. Bar, TV, AC, telephone, minibar, hairdryer, safe, gym. www.mercure.com.*

Le Médiéval €

Located in an 18^{th-}century town house, this 34-room hotel has an excellent location, only three blocks south of the Papal Palace. Decent-sized rooms with beamed ceilings have tub/shower combinations in the bathrooms. Ask for a room on the courtyard rather than the noisy street. *Info: 15 rue Petite Saunerie. Tel. 04/90.86.11.06. V, MC. TV, telephone, hairdryer. www.hotelmedieval.com.*

La Mirande €€€€

This renowned restaurant, located in a hotel in a converted 700-year-old town house behind the Papal Palace, offers elegant French dining. Cooking classes are offered from €95. *Info: 4 place de l'Amirande. Tel. 04/90.14.20.20. Reservations required. www.la-mirande.fr.*

Le 46 €€-€€€

This attractive restaurant is a fine spot for lunch or dinner after visiting the Papal Palace. French cuisine with a Provençal touch. Known for *la plancha de la mer,* featuring shrimp, scallops, and clams. **Le Bar à Vin** (Wine Bar) features wines from throughout France and Europe with an emphasis on local producers. There are usually at least 12 wines by the glass offered (along with cheese-and-meat platters). *Info: 46 rue de la Balance. Tel. 04/90.85.24.83. Closed Sun. No lunch Tue-Thu. www.le46avignon.com.*

Hiély-Lucullus €€€

A lovely and centrally located restaurant serving fine French cuisine, with a Peruvian influence. Try the roasted veal and fresh fish. *Info: 5 rue de la République. Tel. 04/90.86.17.07. Reservations required. Closed Tue and Wed. www.hiely-lucullus.com.*

La Fourchette €€-€€€

French cuisine at this cozy restaurant a block from place de l'Horloge. Try the delicious *suprême de volaille à l'estragon* (chicken breast served in a tarragon sauce). *Info: 17 rue Racine. Tel. 04/90.85.20.93. Closed Sat, Sun, and part of Aug. www.la-fourchette.net.*

Ginette et Marcele €
This cafe is located on a picturesque square. You can dine in the shade or inside surrounded by shelves brimming with bottles of wine and canned Provençal specialties. It's known for its tasty *tartines* (open-faced sandwiches). Our favorite is the *chèvre miel* (goat cheese and honey). Delicious simple salads. *Info: 27 place des Corps Saints (off ue des Lices). Tel. 04/90.85.58.70. Open daily. lepicerie-de-ginette-restaurant-avignon.metro.rest/.*

Avignon Shopping
Les Halles
This large covered market was built in the 1970s. Stinky fish, stinky cheese, and lots of other stuff. There are over 40 stalls here. A great place to gather goods for a cheap meal or picnic. *Info: Place Pie. Tel. 07/63.21.27.54. Open Tue-Sun 6am-2pm. Closed Mon. www.avignon-leshalles.com.*

There is a **flower market** at place des Carmes (Saturday mornings), and a **flea market** at place des Carmes (Sunday mornings).

Pure Lavande/Le Château du Bois
For all your lavender needs! You can purchase cosmetics, beauty supplies, soaps, and gifts all featuring lavender. *Info: 61 rue Grand Fusterie. Tel. 04/90.14.70.05. Open daily. www.lavandeandco.fr.*

Avignon Nighlife & Entertainment
Les Ambassadeurs
Avignon's popular dance club. *Info: 27 rue Bancasse. Tel.04/90.86.31.55. Open Thu-Sat evenings and most evenings before public holidays. www.club-les-ambassadeurs.fr.*

LGBTQ+
Avignon has several gay and gay-friendly establishments:
Le Cid Café: *11 place de l'Horloge. Tel. 04/90.82.30.38 (bar).*
Pub Z: *58 rue de la Bonneterie. Closed Mon. facebook.com/pubz.avignon (bar).*
Sauna Saint Michel: *4 boulevard Saint Michel/Avenue Saint Ruf (Entrée 1). Tel. 04/90.85.06.03 (sauna with bar). facebook.com/hammamstmichel/.*
L'Escave: *12 rue Limas. Tel. 04.90.85.14.91 (bar/club).*

5. LUBERON

HIGHLIGHTS
- The markets, canals, and shops of L'Isle-sur-la-Sorgue
- Fontaine-de-Vaucluse, the "Niagara Falls of Provence"
- The fabulous villages of Gordes, Roussillon, Saignon, and Lourmain
- The lavender fields surrounding Abbaye Notre-Dame de Sénanque

Just a short distance from Avignon and Aix-en-Provence by car, the towns of the **Luberon** region are our favorites. From canals and antique shops in **L'Isle-sur-la-Sorgue** to fine dining in **Lourmarin** to truly unspoiled villages like **Cucuron**, this area offers the perfect vacation. This is the heart of the market area; nearly every town has a great one, and these otherwise quiet towns come to life on market day. The small towns of the Luberon region are just a short distance (20-30 miles [32-48 km]) from Avignon and Aix-en-Provence.

L'Isle-sur-la-Sorgue

L'Isle-sur-la-Sorgue is 16 miles (26 km) east of Avignon/25 miles (40 km) southeast of Orange. L'Isle-sur-la-Sorgue can be reached from Avignon by bus (45 minutes) and by train (30 minutes).

The name means "Island on the Sorgue River," and is often referred to as the "Venice of Provence." We love this valley town. You'll find pedestrian bridges with flower boxes crossing graceful canals. Nine moss-covered waterwheels (that once powered the town's paper, silk, and wool mills) remain along the canals.

Only Paris is said to have more antique and secondhand shops in France. There are more than 300 shops in this little town. Most are open daily. There's a huge antique fair at Easter and mid-August. Antique shops sell everything from furniture to household goods to local art. This otherwise quiet town is filled with crowds on Sunday. Stands loaded with local produce, crafts, and antiques fill the streets along with street performers. *Info: From the place Gambetta (the main entrance to the town) up avenue des 4 Otages.*

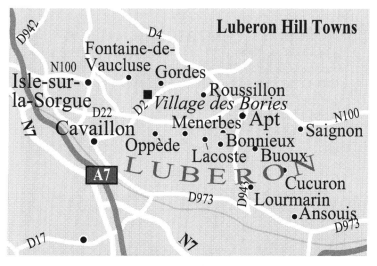

In the center of the Old Town, you'll find the **Collégiale Notre-Dame-des-Anges**, a 17ᵗʰ-century church. Its Baroque interior is filled with gilded statues, frescoes, and faux marble. The highlight are 222 statues of angels shown accompanying the Virgin to heaven. Parts of the church date back to the 12ᵗʰ century. *Info: Center of Old Town. Open daily. Admission: Free.*

Next to the Collégiale Notre-Dame-des-Anges on the place de la Liberté is the picturesque **Café de France**, a good place for a break (€-€€). *Open daily.*

L'Isle-sur-la-Sorgue Sleeping and Eating
La Bastide Rose €€-€€€
This pink villa is located next to a canal. There's a wonderful pool, river views, and an old mill turned into the **Pierre Salinger Museum** (JFK's press secretary, who used to live here). There are five rooms (all have large bathrooms), two suites, and a cottage for rent. *Info: 99 Chemin des Croupières in Le Thor (just outside of town). Tel. 04/90.02.14.33. V, MC, AE. Restaurant, AC, TV, telephone, minibar, in-room safe, hairdryer. www.bastiderose.com.*

The attractive restaurant here, serving fine French and Provençal cuisine, is **Au Gusto/La Table de la Bastide (€€€)**. *Tel. 06/32.64.83.17. Open daily for lunch and dinner. Closed Mon, Tue, and part of Jan. www.au-gusto-restaurant.com.*

Le Café du Village €€
This cafe and restaurant is located in one of the largest and oldest antique centers in the city. Have a light lunch and sip a glass of wine from the Luberon region on the shaded terrace. You'll be surrounded by vendors and shoppers. Just the type of lunch experience you came to Provence for. *Info: 2 bis ave. de l'égalité. Tel. 04/90.15.47.49. Open Fri-Mon. Open Thu in Jul and Aug. www.lecafeduvillage.fr.*

La Prévôte €€€€
Splurge on award-winning cuisine in a lovely setting on a narrow street near the cathedral. Try the excellent *rable de lapin farcis au chèvre* (loin of rabbit stuffed with goat cheese). *Info: 4 bis rue Jean-Jacques-Rousseau. Tel. 04/90.38.57.29. www.la-prevote.fr.*

Also here is **Café Fleurs (€€)** serving traditional and modern French food on its lovely terrace. *Info: Tel. 09/54.12.31.29. Closed Tue and Wed. www.cafefleurs.com.*

The chic **inn (€€-€€€)** here offers five rooms decorated with interesting antiques (which is fitting for this town known for its antique shops). *Info: 4 bis rue Jean-Jacques-Rousseau. Tel. 04/90.38.57.29. V, MC. AC, TV, telephone, safe. www.la-prevote.fr.*

> ## PÉTANQUE
> What game are all those men playing in squares throughout Provence? *Pétanque*, also called *boules*, is played in every Provençal village. A *boule* is a metal ball the size of a baseball. The player who gets his *boule* closest to the target ball (*le cochonnet*) wins. Okay, this is a very simplified version of the game, but you get the picture: French lawn bowling, but it's played on sand!

Le Jardin du Quai €€€

This popular restaurant serves innovative dishes. In good weather, you can dine in its large and lovely garden under chestnut trees. Friendly service. Order the tasty *filet de boeuf* (beef tenderloin). The restaurant also offers cooking classes and has a small shop selling local food specialties and Luberon wines. *Info: 91 avenue Julien Guigue (opposite the station). Tel. 04/90.20.14.98. Closed Tue and Wed. www.jardinduquai.com.*

Fontaine-de-Vaucluse

While nearby L'Isle-sur-la-Sorgue has been called the "Venice of Provence," Fontaine-de-Vaucluse has been called the "Niagara Falls of Provence." It's five miles (eight km) east of L'Isle-sur-la-Sorgue/20 miles (32 km) east of Avignon. Parking €4-€5 on both sides of town.

Don't be disappointed, as at times of the year the *fontaine*, in a cave at the end of a riverside walk, is not much to look at. The best time to see the *fontaine* is in spring and fall. Europe's most powerful spring gushes 55 million gallons (208 million liters) of water each day from the base of 750-feet-high cliffs. The source? No one really knows. Millions visit this sight, and the little village of the same name is loaded with souvenir shops and cafes. You'll pass these on your way to the *fontaine* after you pay to park your car. Visit early or late in the day to avoid the crowds. In the evening, the illuminated *château* sparkles above the town.

While here, there are plenty of cafes and restaurants to take a break. There are also several good special-interest museums. *www.vaucluse.fr.*

The **Musée d'Histoire 1939-1945** is a modern museum devoted to the literature, art, and history of World War II, especially the Nazi occupation of France. *Info: 271 chemin de la Fontaine. Tel. 04/90.20.24.00. Closed Tue, Wed and Oct-Mar. Admission: €7. Currently closed.*

Moulin Vallis-Clausa is a working paper mill where artisans create paper as done in the 15th-century. At the end of your visit, you can make your own sheet of paper. *Info: Chemin de la Fontaine. Tel. 04/90.20.35.44. Open daily 10am-12:30pm and 2pm-6pm (longer hours in summer). Admission: Free. www.moulin-vallisclausa.com.*

Guided **canoe trips** depart from Fontaine-de-Vaucluse on two-hour, five-mile (eight km) trips down the Sorgue River. The trip ends in nearby L'Isle-sur-la-Sorgue and a shuttle brings you back. There are several tour companies offering these trips. One is **Kayaks Verts**, *Tel. 04/82.29.42.42, open mid-May to Sep, from €26, www.canoevaucluse.com.*

Gordes & The Village des Bories

Perched above the Coulon Valley, the small picturesque village of **Gordes** has narrow alleys between stone homes that appear to be stacked on top of each other. *See photo below.* It's 10 miles (16 km) southeast of Fontaine-de-Vaucluse/22 miles (36 km) east of Avignon. Gordes is touristy and trendy, with boutiques and galleries.

In the center of town, you'll find the fortified Renaissance **Château des Gordes**. You can view its interior and a contemporary art collection. *Info: Place Genty Pantaly. Tel. 04/90.72.02.08. Open daily. Admission: Depends on exhibit.*

Also in the center of town is the **Eglise St-Firmin**. Stop in for a quick view of the church's blue floral interior and faux marble pulpit. *Info: Rue du Belvédère. Open daily. Admission: Free.*

The **Caves du Palais St-Firmin** are underground passages and cellars that you can explore. A small museum allows you to discover the different uses of the cellars. There are frequent wine tastings offered. *Info: Rue du Belvédère. Tel. 07/61.44.93.12. Open daily Apr-Oct. Admission: €6. www.caves-saint-firmin.com.*

Only two miles (3.2 km) away from Gordes is a popular tourist destination, the **Village des Bories**. Bories are beehive-shaped stone huts built by peasants (without mortar) who lived in them while tending their flocks. There are said to be 6,000 in Provence. It's believed that Neolithic man lived in huts like these, and that they were copied over the years. This cluster of bories is part of a village showcasing this peasant community, which was inhabited between 1600 and 1800. Note that if you're unable to park in the lot closest to the village, the walk from route D2 is 1.2 miles (two km). *Info: Two miles (3.2 km) southwest of Gordes off route D2 toward Coustellet. Tel. 04/90.72.03.48. Open daily 9am until sunset. Admission: €6. www.levillagedesbories.com.*

Gordes Sleeping & Eating
La Bastide €€€

This 45-unit inn–suites are the most expensive–is located in one of the stone homes that appear to be stacked on top of each other here. Tastefully decorated rooms, attentive staff, and a luxurious pool all make this a perfect base to explore the area. *Info: 61 rue de la Combe. Tel. 04/90.72.12.12. V, MC, AE. Restaurant, bar, gym, AC, TV, telephone, minibar, in-room safe, hairdryer. www.bastide-de-gordes.com.*

L'Outsider €€-€€€

Provençal and Mediterranean dishes on the lovely terrace or insider under stone vaulted walls. Attentive staff. The specialty here is *gigot d'agneau grillé et son jus au romarin* (grilled leg of lamb in a rosemary sauce). *Info: Rue de la Gendarmerie. Tel. 04/32.50.27.52. Closed Tue and Wed lunch. www.restaurant-loutsider.com.*

La Trinquette €€-€€€

Modern French cuisine, using local producers, is served on the lovely terrace in good weather. Garlic mayonnaise (*aïoli*), a Provençal specialty, is featured in many dishes. Start with the *salade d'artichauts* (artichoke salad) and do not miss the shrimp ravioli. *Info: Rue des Tracapelles. Tel. 04/90.72.11.62. Dinner served Thu-Mon. Closed Tue and Wed.*

Only two miles (3.2 km) from Gordes is a must-see sight and worth the drive. If you're visiting in late June, July, or August, the lavender fields surrounding the austere 12th-century abbey **Abbaye Notre-Dame de Sénanque** are in splendid bloom. *See photo on page 46.* Even if you don't visit the abbey, don't miss this perfect photo opportunity. You can visit the cloisters, church, refectory, and dormitory. The only heated room was the calefactory, or sitting room, which allowed the monks to read and write without freezing. There are permanent exhibits on the history of the Cistercians and the construction of the abbey, and there are still monks who make this their home. *Info: Two miles (3.2 km) north of Gordes on route D177. Tel. 04/90.72.18.24. Open Mon-Sat 9:45am-11am and 1pm-5pm, Sun 1pm-5pm. Admission: €8.50. Guided tours at www.senanque.fr.*

COLORFUL LAVENDER

It's everywhere and it's beautiful. During lavender season (late June through August), there's nothing more breathtaking than lavender fields and yellow fields of sunflowers. Lavender is harvested beginning in July and distilled for perfume and soap. Some of the most spectacular lavender fields are found between Buoux and Forcalquier. For those interested in lavender, you can visit the **Musée de la Lavande** on route D2 in Cabrières outside of Gordes. *Info: Tel. 04/90.76.91.23. Open daily. Closed Jan. Admission: €8 (includes English audioguide). www.museedelalavande.com.*

Roussillon

Today, we'll visit colorful **Roussillon** (*see photo on next page*) and experience a taste of old Provence in Oppède-le-Vieux. Roussillon is six miles (10 km) east of Gordes/28 miles (45 km) east of Avignon.

Legend has it that a local lord had his wife's lover killed and the wife threw herself off a cliff, staining the rocks with her blood. In reality, two centuries of ochre mining have left this perched village surrounded by red quarries and cliffs. From deep red to light yellow, the colors of this town alone are worth a visit. Although it can be quite crowded in high tourist season, you can still find peaceful, beautiful squares and take in the surrounding countryside.

The Sentier des Ocres (Ochre Trail)

Two circular trails (30 minutes and 50 minutes) in the village have signs that highlight local flora and the history of ochre mining. The peaceful walks take you through chestnut and pine groves. Admission: €3.50.

Domaine de Tara

Located less than a mile northwest of Roussillon, this winery has a tasting room where you can sample wines from its vineyard. Lovely setting facing the Monts du Vaucluse, Mont Ventoux, and the village of Gordes. *Info: Les Rossignols. 2005 Route de Gordes. Off D102 on the road to Joucas. Tel. 04/90.05.74.87. Open daily 10am-7:30pm. www.domainedetara.com.*

Roussillon Sleeping & Eating

Omma/Le Clos de la Glycine €€

Located in the heart of the village, this comfortable nine-room inn is a great choice. Rooms are charming and most have sweeping views of the ochre cliffs. *Info: place de la Poste. Tel. 04/90.05.60.13. V, MC. AC, TV, minibar, safe, hairdryer. www.leclosdelaglycine.fr.*

Restaurant David €€€

Provençal specialties are served at this attractive restaurant located at Le Clos de la Glycine inn (*see above*) in the heart of Roussillon. The restaurant has panoramic views and a terrace overlooking the ochre cliffs. Try the *filet d'agneau de pays rôti* (roasted baked lamb filet) or *cochon* (pork) served with asparagus. *Info: Place de la Poste. Tel. 04/90.05.60.13. Closed Mon and Tue in Mar, Apr, Oct, and Nov. www.leclosdelaglycine.fr.*

Le Piquebaure €€€

Indoor and outdoor dining at this restaurant serving Provençal classics, such as such as grilled *entrecôte*. End your meal with the delicious lavender *crème brûlée*. You'll enjoy the view of the countryside from the terrace. *Info:167 Avenue Dame Sirmonde. Tel. 04/32.52.94.48. Dinner only. Closed Wed. lerestaurantlepiquebaure.business.site.*

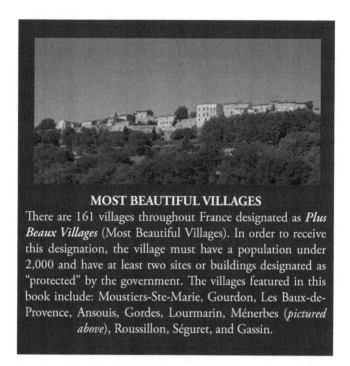

MOST BEAUTIFUL VILLAGES
There are 161 villages throughout France designated as *Plus Beaux Villages* (Most Beautiful Villages). In order to receive this designation, the village must have a population under 2,000 and have at least two sites or buildings designated as "protected" by the government. The villages featured in this book include: Moustiers-Ste-Marie, Gourdon, Les Baux-de-Provence, Ansouis, Gordes, Lourmarin, Ménerbes (*pictured above*), Roussillon, Séguret, and Gassin.

Just three miles (five km) southeast of Roussillon on route D108 is the **Pont Julien**. This three-arched bridge was built by the Romans over 2,000 years ago without the use of mortar. It crosses the Calavon River.

While Roussillon is usually crowded with tourists, the nearby town of **Oppède-le-Vieux** will give you a taste of Old Provence. It's nine miles (14 km) south of Gordes/16 miles (26 km) southeast of Avignon. This hilltop village (don't confuse it with the lower modern town of Oppède), surrounded by thick forests, was deserted in 1900. The ruins of a medieval *château* loom above. In fact, much of the town itself is still in ruins, although some artists and writers have moved in and beautifully restored homes. You must park at the base of the hill (€3) and walk through a tiered garden filled with local plants labeled with their Latin, French, and English names. Cross through the old city gate and walk up the steep alleys to visit the 13th-century church **Notre-Dame d'Alydon**, with its gargoyles and hexagon-shaped bell tower. Truly a taste of old Provence.

Outside the old city gate, you can stop for a drink or a bite at the attractive **Le Petit Café des Jeanne**. Try the *charcuterie* with beef and Iberian pork or the leek gratin with curry and shrimp. *Info: 12 rue Sainte-Cécile. Tel. 04/90.76.74.01. Closed Mon. www.lepetitcafedesjeanne.fr.*

Ménerbes & The Land of *A Year in Provence*

Peter Mayle wrote *A Year in Provence* about **Ménerbes** and the towns surrounding it. Ménerbes is three miles (five km) east of Oppède-le-Vieux/19 miles (31 km) southeast of Avignon.

This town, with its impressive fortifications and crowned by the turreted *château*, was once a Protestant stronghold during the 16th-century War of the Religions. You'll find Renaissance homes and terrific views of the countryside. Visit the attractive **place de l'Horloge** (Clock Square), in the shadow of City Hall. Although Picasso once owned a home in Ménerbes, it's another home that gets all the attention. Peter Mayle wrote the enormously successful *A Year in Provence* about his home and the towns surrounding it. Tour buses still pass by and gawk. He no longer lives here and it's hard to feel sorry for the current owners as they must have known what they were getting themselves into! *Info: One mile (1.6 km) from Ménerbes on route D3 to Bonnieux (second house from the right after the soccer field). No admission.*

Between Oppède-le-Vieux and Ménerbes is the **Musée du Tire-Bouchon** (Corkscrew Museum). Housed in a mansion, this museum doesn't just feature thousands of corkscrews. It also has wine tastings. *Info: 601 route de Cavaillon. On route D109 between Oppède-le-Vieux and Ménerbes. Tel. 04/90.72.41.58. Closed weekends in winter. Admission: €5. www.museedutirebouchon.com.*

Just four miles (six km) east of Ménerbes is **Lacoste**. This town, with its fortified medieval gateways, is dominated by the *château* that was once owned by the Marquis de Sade who hosted his infamous orgies here. The castle was restored by designer Pierre Cardin. The town comes to life in late July and August when the **Festival Lacoste**, with musical and theatrical events, takes place. *www.festivaldelacoste.com.*

When visiting this area, don't miss the hilltop village of **Bonnieux.**

It's three miles (five km) east of Lacoste/ seven miles (11 km) southeast of Roussillon/28 miles (46 km) northwest of Aix-en-Provence.

Layers of homes topped with a 12th-century church (the simply named Vieille Eglise or "Old Church") make Bonnieux one of the most impressive hilltop villages. Its steep streets are bordered by restored homes. Climb the 86 steps from the place de la Liberté and rue de la Mairie up to the church to take in the sweeping view of the surrounding countryside.

If you want to visit one of Peter Mayle's favorites in *A Year in Provence*, head to the small town of **Buoux**, five miles (nine km) south of Apt. This peaceful rural town is surrounded by lavender fields and crowned by the ruins of the Buoux Fort.

Buoux Sleeping & Eating
Auberge des Seguins €-€€
This rustic inn is located in a 16th-century stone building six miles (9.6 km) from Apt. It features an outdoor swimming pool with a terrace restaurant and bar serving Provençal specialties. Rooms are basic and you have the option of having your evening meal and breakfast included in the room rate. Guests can access hiking trails from the property. *Info: Combe De Lourmarin Les Seguins 84480 in Buoux. Tel. 04/90.74.16.37. Restaurant opened daily for lunch and dinner (menu €28). Inn and restaurant open from Apr-Nov 15. www.aubergedesseguins.com.*

Apt & Saignon

Apt is 32 miles (52 km) northwest of Aix-en-Provence/32 miles (52 km) west of Avignon.

Apt's claim to fame, despite its unattractive industrial outskirts, is that it's the world capital of candied fruit (*fruits-confits*). You'll find shops selling it everywhere. The Old Town (**Vieille Ville**) with its narrow streets is worth a visit. The **Cathédrale Ste-Anne** (closed Sunday afternoons) in the Old Town has a large collection of relics (guided tours only), and the cathedral's crypt is said to hold the remains of St. Anne, the mother of the Virgin Mary.

There's a huge market on Saturday mornings at place de la Bouquerie. Especially good for purchasing candied fruit (*fruits-confits*), for which the town is known.

Nearby is the truly unspoiled hill town of **Saignon**. It's two miles (3.2 km) southeast of Apt. Out of the way, but certainly worth the trip!

This lovely, quiet, and unspoiled town high on a hill has picturesque shady squares, time-worn fountains, and ruins of ancient baths. The wood-carved doors of the Roman church **Eglise Notre-Dame de Pitié** depict Christ and Mary. The cemetery behind the church provides its permanent "residents" with a panoramic view of the countryside.

Lourmarin

Hungry? Head to **Lourmarin**, the gastronomic capital of Provence. It's six miles (10 km) south of Bonnieux.

Lourmarin's winding narrow streets are lined with stone houses painted in shades of ochre and beige. It has a Renaissance chapel and both Catholic and Protestant churches. The village lies at the foot of the Luberon Mountain range which is covered with pine and oak trees. Surrounding the village are olive groves and vineyards. Although French vacationers discovered this little village years ago, it's now popular with foreign tourists. Its renovated *château* is the site of frequent concerts and exhibits. Visitors have quite a few cafes and restaurants to choose from, and it's become the gastronomic capital of the area. It's a lovely town with much to offer, and a great base for touring some of the prettiest towns of Provence.

There's a Friday-morning market in Lourmarin.

Head to **Les Caves du Château**. The interesting wines of the Côtes du Luberon, along with regional products, are available at this shop under the *château*. Friendly and helpful staff and generous wine tastings. *Info: Avenue Raoul Dautry. Tel. 06/10.69.09.26. Open daily in high season.*

Lourmarin Sleeping and Eating
Les Olivettes €€€
You can rent an apartment in a renovated farmhouse in the Lu-beron. It has spectacular views, a large heated swimming-pool, private gardens and, most of all, a relaxing and peaceful atmo-sphere. It's an ideal base for visiting the villages of the Luberon. Perfect for large families and groups. *Info: Avenue Henri Bosco (off route 27). Tel. 06/21.58.45.41. Weekly rental from €1300. V, MC. Outdoor pool. Kitchen, TV, telephone. www.olivettes.com.*

Le Moulin €€
This hotel is located in a 17th-century building. The 17 rooms and two suites are decorated with local pottery and Provençal furni-ture. You can relax in the attractive lounge near the fireplace or on the terrace. *Info: Avenue Raoul Dautry. Tel. 04/90.68.06.69. V, MC. Each room has different amenities, including AC, TV, minibar, safe, hairdryer. www.beaumier.com.*

The restaurant here (€€€) serves French and Provençal dishes. Try the *côte de veau* (veal chop) served in a sage sauce or the *cochon fermier servi rosé* (free range pork served in a rosé sauce). You'll dine in a lovely room with vaulted ceilings and stone walls. *Info: Closed Mon and Tue.*

Le Comptoir €€-€€€
This cafe and restaurant serves Italian and Provençal dishes on a lovely square in the middle of town. An excellent place to have a light lunch and sip a glass of local rosé. Try the delicious *fleurs des courgettes farcies* (zucchini flowers stuffed with cheese). *Info: Place Barthélémy/Monté du Galnier. Tel. 04/90.08.49.13. Open daily.*

Auberge La Fenière €€€-€€€€
This restaurant and inn was established by Chef Reine Sammut, the "Queen of Provençal cooking." Experience innovative dishes at this restaurant on the outskirts of town. *Info: Route de Cadenet (D943). Tel. 04/90.68.11.79. Closed Mon, Tue, and Jan. www.aubergelafeniere.com.*

The inn here (€€-€€€) has stylish rooms housed in several different buildings on the estate. Lush gardens and a beautiful pool! *Info: AC, TV, parking.*

There are two towns nearby that are worth the short drives. **Cucuron** is only four miles (seven km) east of Lourmarin. Tourism has yet to invade this scenic small town. Parts of the ancient walls survive. A fortified gate and bell tower on place de l'Horloge is the entry for the ruins above the town. Take a break with locals at cafes along the large stone pool (**Bassin de l'Etang**) dating back to the 15th century. There's a large market here on Tuesday mornings. The church **Eglise Notre-Dame-de-Beaulieu** has Gothic chapels and a Baroque altarpiece. Near the church is an ancient olive press, **Moulin à Huile Dauphin**, with a shop selling local specialties.

Ansouis is only eight miles (10 km) southeast of Lourmarin; the town lies at the foot of its medieval castle. The village houses are spread over the southern slope to shelter them from the Mistral (the brutal winds that touch this area at certain times of the year). There's a 16th-century tower crowned with a wrought-iron bell tower, and the castle with its fortified walls and watchtower has been restored (guided visits only in the afternoons). Wooded groves, gardens, and terraces surround the castle.

You can pop into the church **Eglise St-Martin**. Originally a 12th-century fortress and former law court, this small church contains 17th- and 18th-century statues and altar pieces. At the entry to the castle, you can stop into the information center and purchase an inexpensive bottle of local wine. There's a market on Sunday mornings.

Avid gardeners will want to visit **La Ferme de Gerbaud**, a 62-acre farm on the slopes of the Luberon mountain range, offering 90-minute guided tours in English and French. You'll see aromatic herbs and regional plants. The shop sells fragrances, dyes, olive oils, and herbs. *Info: Two miles (3.2 km) outside of Lourmarin (chemin d'Aguye to chemin de Gerbaud). Tel. 06/45.42.57.12. Tours Apr-Oct Tue, Thu, and Sat at 5pm, Nov-Mar Sun at 3pm. Admission: €5. www.plantes-aromatiques-provence.com.*

6. AIX-EN-PROVENCE

HIGHLIGHTS
- A walk down the cours Mirabeau,
Aix's lovely main street
- Quartier Mazarin, filled with elegant townhouses
- The huge market at place Verdun
- Musée Granet, home
to a collection of Cézanne paintings

Aix (pronounced "X") is a graceful and sophisticated city. Between the 12th and 15th centuries it was the capital of Provence. The Romans called it "Aquae Sextius" (Waters of Sextius) after the thermal springs that flow here and the Roman general (Caius Sextius Calvinus) who founded the city.

Shaded squares with bubbling fountains in the Old Quarter, 17th-century town houses, and the **cours Mirabeau** (the grand main avenue) make Aix a must for all visitors to Provence. It's a cultural center enhanced by thousands of students who attend one of France's oldest universities. It's the hometown of the artist **Paul Cézanne**, who created many of his best-known works here.

Aix-en-Provence (population 142,000) is in the south of France. It's 19 miles (31 km) northeast of the Mediterranean port city of Marseille, 51 miles (82k m) southeast of Avignon, and 474 miles (760 km) south of Paris. The tourist office and parking areas are at place Général-de-Gaulle. Aix has a TGV (fast-speed train) station on the edge of town. For more information on train travel to Aix, see the *Planning Your Trip* section.

Sights
La Rotonde
The black-and-white marble fountain at place Général-de-Gaulle (in the middle of the traffic circle) dates back to the 19th century, and features the figures of Fine Art, Agriculture, and Justice at the top.

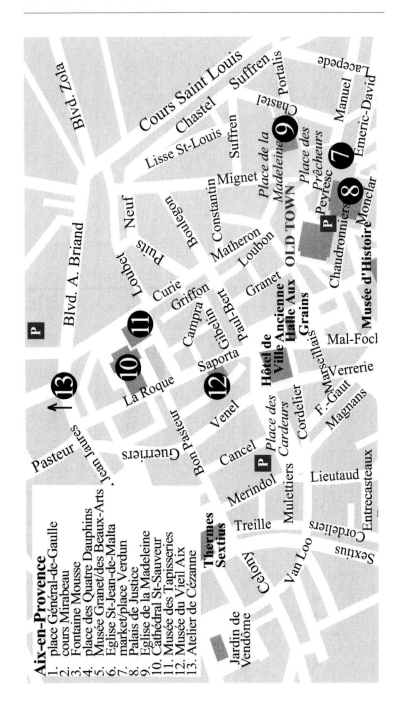

Aix-en-Provence
1. place Général-de-Gaulle
2. cours Mirabeau
3. Fontaine Mousse
4. place des Quatre Dauphins
5. Musée Granet/des Beaux-Arts
6. Eglise St-Jean-de-Malta
7. market/place Verdun
8. Palais de Justice
9. Eglise de la Madeleine
10. Cathédral St-Sauveur
11. Musée des Tapisseries
12. Musée du Vieil Aix
13. Atelier de Cézanne

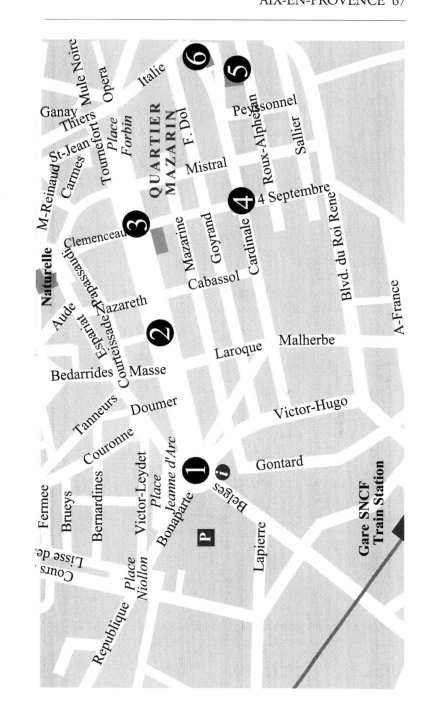

Cours Mirabeau

This broad street lined with plane trees and stone buildings was built in the 17th century. You'll pass elegant buildings, four fountains, and many cafes and shops. This is the heart of Aix. One of the grand mansions on this street, the impressive **Hôtel Maurel de Pontèves** (now the Tribunal of Commerce) with its sculpted figures is at number 38. *See photo on page 73.* In the middle of the cours Mirabeau is the **Fontaine Moussue** (it means "Mossy Fountain"–you'll understand why when you see it). The formal name of this fountain is **Fontaine d'Eau Chaude** (Hot Water Fountain).

Quartier Mazarin

It was here that Aix nobility built elegant town houses in the 17th and 18th centuries. **Place des Quatre Dauphins** is dominated by a Baroque fountain. The elegant 17th-century **Fontaine des Quatre Dauphins** (Four Dolphins Fountain) features four dolphins at the base of a pine cone-topped obelisk. *Info: If you exit the cours Mirabeau on to rue du 4 Septembre, you'll enter the Quartier Mazarin.*

Musée Granet

One sight of interest in the Quartier Mazarin is located in a former priory and is home to a collection of European art from the 16th to 19th centuries. You'll find a collection of Cézanne paintings here, along with his drawings and watercolors. Interesting exhibitions have included the works of David Hockney. *Info: Place St-Jean-de-Malte on rue Cardinale. Tel. 04/42.52.88.32. Open noon-6pm (Jun-Sep 10am-6pm). Closed Mon. Admission: €6.50. www.museegranet-aixenprovence.fr.*

Eglise St-Jean-de-Malte

This Gothic church and chapel of the Knights of Malta (a charitable organization) is home to the tombs of the counts of Provence. Also here is *The Crucifixion* by Delacroix. Drop in for a quick view. It's located next to the Musée Granet. *Info: Rue Cardinale and rue d'Italie. Open daily. Admission: Free.*

Festival d'Aix is held in late June and early July. World-class opera productions are held in the courtyard of the Palais de l'Archevêché and other venues throughout the city. www.festival-aix.com.

Place Verdun

This square in Old Town is home to the grand **Palais de Justice** (Palace of Justice) which was completed in 1831. On the adjoining place des Prêcheurs is the **Eglise de la Madeleine**. Formerly a Dominican convent, this Baroque church is the site of frequent classical concerts. *Info: Place des Prêcheurs (off place de la Madeleine). Open daily. Admission: Free.*

If you're here on Tuesday, Thursday, or Saturday mornings, you'll run into a huge market. You'll find clothes, antiques, and produce at the colorful **Aix Market** held in place de Verdun and place des Prêcheurs. From place Verdun, you'll find the **Passage Agard** (it has the words "Agard" written above it). It's a covered passageway lined with shops. The *passage* connects the place Verdun with the cours Mirabeau.

Cathédral St-Sauveur

On the rue Gaston-de-Saporta (the heart of Old Town), this cathedral has a 5th-century baptistery, 12th-century cloisters, and a 15th-century triptych (three-paneled painting), *The Burning Bush*. The famous triptych is only open for special occasions, however, to protect it from further deterioration. Near the triptych is another three-paneled painting of Christ's passion. The fantastic organ is Baroque, and the tapestries surrounding the choir date from the 18th century. *Info: rue Gaston-de-Saporta at place des Martyrs de la Résistance. Open daily. Admission: Free. www.cathedrale-aix.net.*

Musée des Tapisseries

This 17th-century archbishop's palace is home to a museum of 17th- and 18th-century tapestries and furnishings. There are 17 hangings and a series on the life of Don Quixote. It's located next to the cathedral. *Info: 28 place des Martyrs de la Résistance. Tel. 04/42.23.09.91. Open April 15-Oct 15 10am-12:30pm and 1:30pm-6pm (until 5pm Oct 14-Apr 14). Closed Tue. Admission: €4. www.aixenprovence.fr/musee-des-tapisseries.*

Musée Estienne de Saint-Jean/Musée du Vieil Aix

This beautiful 17th-century mansion is more interesting than the museum of eclectic furniture and objects it houses. *Info: 17 rue Gaston-de-Saporta. Tel. 04/88.71.74.31. Open April 15-Oct 15 10am-12:30pm and 1:30pm-6pm (until 5pm Oct 14-Apr 14). Closed Tue and Jan. Admission: €4.*

Atelier de Cézanne

The artist Paul Cézanne is from Aix, and created many of his best-known works here. You can visit his studio, the Atelier de Cézanne. It's located just north of the Old Town. Americans paid to have his studio restored, and you'll find it much like he left it in 1906. *Info: 9 avenue Paul-Cézanne. Tel. 04/42.21.06.53. Open Tue-Sat mid-Jan-Mar and Oct-Dec 9:30am-12:30pm and 2pm-5pm (Closed Sun and Mon), Apr-May daily 9:30am-12:30pm and 2pm-6pm, June-Sep daily 9:30am-6pm. Admission: €6.50. Tours in English at 3:30pm for €9.50. Also at 10am Jul-Aug. www.cezanne-en-provence.com.*

Aix Sleeping & Eating
Hotel Cézanne €€-€€€
This modern, chic hotel has fun and eclectic décor. There are 55 rooms and 12 suites. Its location near the train station makes it a great place to stay if you plan to venture out to other towns in Provence. Tasty, large brunch is served daily. The only thing it lacks is a pool. *Info: 40 avenue Victor Hugo. Tel. 04/42.91.11.11. V, MC, AE. Bar, AC, TV, telephone, minibar, safe. boutiquehotelcezanne.com.*

Villa Gallici €€€
A stylish and sumptuous hotel located on a secluded lane in a residential area, just a short walk from the cours Mirabeau. Many of the 22 rooms have their own patios. Pleasant outdoor pool. *Info: Avenue de la Violette. Tel. 04/42.23.29.23. V, MC, AE. Restaurant, bar, AC, TV, telephone, minibar, safe. www.villagallici.com.*

Hôtel Nègrecoste €€
Smack dab in the middle of the cours Mirabeau, this traditional hotel has 35 rooms and is certainly worth considering. Rooms are medium-sized and have soundproof windows. Some have nice views of the cours Mirabeau, Aix's main street. *Info: 33 cours Mirabeau. Tel. 04/42.27.74.22. V, MC, AE. AC, TV, minibar, hairdyer, safe. www.hotelnegrecoste.com.*

Hôtel Cardinal €-€€
Located in the Quartier Mazarin filled with elegant town houses, this 29-room hotel (and nearby annex) is a good value with basic, comfortable rooms, a helpful staff, and a great location. Note that with no air-conditioning, rooms can be hot in summer. *Info: 24 rue Cardinale. Tel. 04/42.38.32.30. V, MC. TV, hairdyer. www.hotel-cardinal-aix.com.*

Hôtel des Quatre Dauphins €€
Also located in the quiet Quartier Mazarin, this small, 13-room hotel is another good value with basic, comfortable accommodations and a fine location. *Info: 54 rue Roux-Alphéran. Tel. 04/42.38.16.39. V, MC. TV. www.hotel-aix-lesquatredauphins.fr.*

La Fromagerie du Passage €€

This restaurant, wine shop, and cheese shop is located in the Passage Agard (a covered passageway that connects place Verdun with the cours Mirabeau). The highlight here are the cheese platters paired with Provençal wines from €28. This is also a great place for lunch as they serve excellent sandwiches. You can dine on the rooftop terrace. *Info: Passage Agard/55 cours Mirabeau. Tel. 04/42.22.90.00. Closed Mon. lafromageriedupassage.com.*

Le Saint-Estève €€€€

This award-winning restaurant is located at the Hôtel Les Lodges Sainte-Victoire (€€€). Both the restaurant and hotel opened in 2013 on ten acres about a ten-minute drive from Aix. You'll dine on innovative French cuisine with a view of the surrounding vineyards and olive groves. This is one of Provence and the French Riviera's best places to dine. *Info: 2250 route de Cézanne in Le Tholonet. Tel. 04/42.24.80.40. Closed Mon Sep-Apr. Reservations required. Fixed-priced menus from €140. www.leslodgessaintevictoire.com.*

Aux Petits Oignons €

Tired of all that French food? This small and attractive eatery (near place des Prêcheurs) serves burgers, hot dogs, and crispy French fries. There are always vegan and vegetarian options. No seating inside, but there are a few tables outside. Fantastic desserts and many are gluten free. Friendly service. *Info: 2 rue Peyresc. Tel. 06/18.19.00.96. Closed Sat. www.comptoirgourmand.net.*

Aix Shopping

Aix is one of the best cities in Provence to shop. You'll find fashionable clothing shops (especially on rue Fabrot), Provençal fabric shops (rue Marius Reinaud), and shops selling *calissons d'Aix*, a candy made from ground almonds, melon, and fruit syrup (**Béchard** at 12 cours Mirabeau. Closed Sun and Mon).

Nightlife & Entertainment
Casino Aix

If you're tired of museums and cafes, try your luck at the casino. There's also a restaurant here. *Info: 21 avenue de l'Europe. Tel. 04/42.59.69.00. Open daily. Slot machines from 10am. Gaming tables from 3pm. www.casinoaix.com.*

Sports & Recreation
Château l'Arc Golf Club

This prestigious golf club is located in nearby Fuveau, only seven miles (12 km) from Aix. Challenging 18-hole course. *Info: Domaine Château l'Arc (route D6). Tel. 04/42.29.83.43. www.chateaularcgolfclub.com.*

7. ARLES

HIGHLIGHTS
- Roman ruins
- Espace Van Gogh
- Old Town in St. Rémy
- Les Baux-de-Provence, a delightful
medieval hilltop village with splendid views
- Flamingos and birds in the
Parc Regional de Camargue

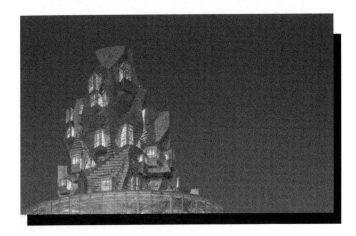

On the banks of the Rhône River, **Arles** is one of the three "A's" that make up the most visited cities in Provence (along with Aix-en-Provence and Avignon). Arles has everything you could want in a Provence city: festivals, an Old Town, Roman ruins, cafes (especially on place du Forum), and intimate restaurants.

Since Arles is situated at the head of the Rhône delta, it's on the route that linked Italy and Spain. When the Romans came into possession of Spain, Arles became an important and strategic town for them. Bullfights, still held in the arena, are a reminder of Arles's Spanish connection. The folk culture and traditions of Arles are alive and well, and you'll see locals dressed in traditional Arlesian costumes on special occasions. **Van Gogh** came here in 1888 and created some of his best-known paintings. Look around and you'll notice that many of the scenes featured in those paintings remain today.

Arles (population 53,000) is in the south of France. It's 57 miles (92 km) inland from the Mediterranean port city of Marseille, 22 miles (36 km) south of Avignon, and 450 miles (752 km) south of Paris. Arles can be reached from Avignon by bus (90 minutes) and by train (20 minutes). The train station and bus station in Arles are located next to each other.

Sights
Espace van Gogh
This is where Vincent van Gogh was sent after he is said to have cut off part of his left ear. The courtyard, which is open to the public, has been landscaped to match van Gogh's famous painting *Le Jardin de l'Hôtel-Dieu*. The building was formerly a hospital. Today it's a cultural center with a wing dedicated to van Gogh that houses an art exhibit. *Info: Place Dr. Félix Ray. Open daily. Admission: Free.*

Place du Forum
There are many cafes at this attractive square, including **Café de la Nuit**. It's the one that looks like a vibrant van Gogh painting. Great people-watching here!

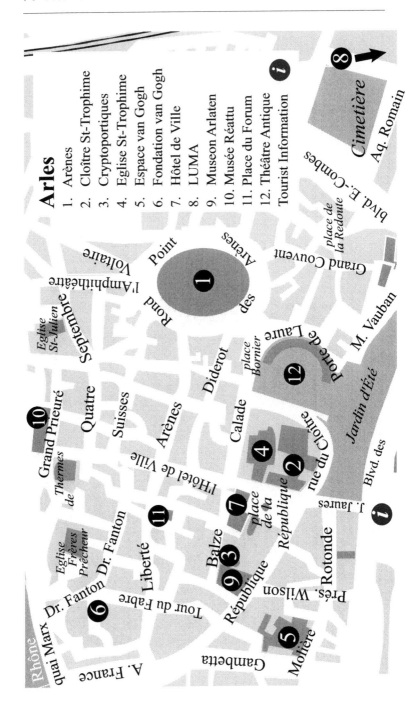

Arles

1. Arènes
2. Cloître St-Trophime
3. Cryptoportiques
4. Eglise St-Trophime
5. Espace van Gogh
6. Fondation van Gogh
7. Hôtel de Ville
8. LUMA
9. Museon Arlaten
10. Musée Réattu
11. Place du Forum
12. Théâtre Antique
    Tourist Information

Fondation van Gogh

This van Gogh-themed gallery has no permanent collection. The gallery exhibits works of major contemporary artists paying homage to van Gogh in re-creations of his works. There is usually only one van Gogh painting here (or for that matter in all of Arles). The foundation is known for its contemporary architecture and design. You'll want to visit the rooftop terrace and check out the colored glass on the ceiling of the bookstore. When van Gogh and fellow painter Paul Gauguin worked together in Arles in 1888, they were treated rather badly. This gallery seems to be an attempt to correct that wrong. *Info: 35 rue du Docteur Fanton. Tel. 04/88.65.82.93. Open daily 10am-6pm. Admission: €10. www.fondation-vincentvangogh-arles.org.*

Musée Réattu

This art museum is named after Provençal artist Jacques Réattu. In addition to his works and some 16th-century tapestries, you'll find drawings, etchings, and paintings by such notables as Picasso and Gauguin. *Info: 10 rue du Grand Prieuré. Tel. 04/90.49.37.58. Open 10am-6pm (Nov-Feb until 5pm). Closed Mon. Admission: €6. www.museereattu.arles.fr.*

Place de la République

The main square in Arles. Take in the City Hall (**Hôtel de Ville**) dating back to the 1600s. The **obelisk** with its carved features is thought to have been a trophy from the conquest of Egypt by Rome during the reign of Emperor Augustus.

LUMA Arles

This art center is the home of the LUMA Foundation. It's housed in a 10-story tower designed by famous architect Frank Gehry. Gehry's inspiration for the building was Vincent van Gogh. He hoped to catch the light that the artists sought in Arles. The tower features thousands of angled, reflective stainless steel panels. The building includes a library, an auditorium, exhibition spaces, and a cafe. *See photo on bottom of page 74. Info: 35 avenue Victor Hugo (in the Parc des Ateliers). Tel. 04/65.88.10.00. Open Wed-Mon 10am-6pm. Closed Tue. Admission: Free. www.luma.org.*

Eglise St-Trophime/Cloître St-Trophime

The vivid frieze of the Last Judgment in the doorway, a Roman sarcophagus, and the cloisters are masterpieces of medieval architecture. The recently restored portal shows Christ with life-sized apostles in the columns below. *Info: Place de la République. Tel. 04/90.49.59.05. Open daily 9am-6pm. Admission: Free. €6 to the cloister.*

Cryptoportiques

If your time is limited, you may want to skip this sight. No one is really certain of the purpose these ancient underground crypts served, which date back to 46 BC. In World War II, they harbored the French Resistance. *Info: Rue Balze. Tel. 04/90.49.36.74. Open daily Nov-Feb 10am-5pm; Mar, Apr and Oct 9am-6pm; May-Sep 9am-7pm. Admission: €4.50.*

Museon Arlaten (Arles Museum)

The folk culture and traditions of Arles are alive and well at this recently renovated museum. Women in traditional costumes watch over you as you view regional clothes, furniture, portraits, and art objects. The museum has a room dedicated to Frédéric Mistral, a poet from Provence who was awarded the 1904 Nobel Prize in Literature. Since the museum is dedicated to preserving Provençal culture, the descriptions are in French and the Provençal language. An app is available in English. *Info: 29 rue de la République. Tel. 04/13.31.51.99. Open Tue-Sun 9:30am-6pm. Closed Mon. Admission: €8. www.museonarlaten.fr.*

Musée de l'Arles Antique (Museum of Ancient Arles)

This modern, blue, triangular museum is located on the site of a huge Roman chariot-racing stadium (*cirque*). Mosaics, sculptures, and detailed models of ancient monuments as they existed are all on view here. Most come to see the world's most famous collection of carved sarcophagi. *Info: Presqu'île du Cirque Romain (1.5 mile [.8 km] outside of the center city). Tel. 04/13.31.51.03. Open Wed-Mon 10am to 6pm. Closed Tue. Admission: €8. English tours at 3pm on Thu Jul-Aug. www.arlesantique.fr.*

Théâtre Antique

Arles has two important Roman ruins. This ancient theatre is used today as a stage for festivals. It was built in the 1st century and seated 10,000. All that remains are two columns. You can pretty much see all of it by looking over the fence from rue du Cloître. *Info: Rue de la Calade. Tel. 04.90.18.41.20. Open daily May-Sep 9am-7pm, Mar, Apr, and Oct 9am-6pm, Nov-Feb 10:30am-4:30pm. Admission: €9. Combined tickets fro Arles monuments at www.arlestourisme.com.*

Arènes

The highlight of your trip to Arles will likely be a visit to one of the most spectacular Roman monuments in Provence. *See photo on page 74.* The well-preserved arena with its two tiers of arches and four medieval towers once held over 20,000 spectators. It still hosts bullfights. Some are the traditional gory type and others are "Provence style" where the bull isn't killed. Much of the original structure remains, including terraces, galleries, and even its original drainage system. *Info: Rond Point des Arènes. Tel. 08/91.70.03.70. Open daily May-Sep 9am-7pm, Mar, Apr, and Oct 9am-6pm, Nov-Feb 10:30am-4:30pm. Admission: €9. www.arlestourisme.com and www.arennes-arles.com.*

Abbaye de Montmajour

The ruins of this massive Romanesque abbey sit in the middle of marshland north of Arles. You can visit the now vacant abbey and its peaceful cloister. Van Gogh came here often to paint. *Info: Three miles (five km) northeast of Arles on route D17. Tel. 04/90.54.64.17. Open daily 10am-5pm (until 6:30pm Jun-Sep). Closed Mon Oct-Mar. Admission: €6. www.abbaye-montmajour.fr.*

Les Alyscamps

If you have time, you can squeeze in a visit to one of the world's most famous cemeteries, to see Greek, Roman, and Christian tombs. *Info: Rue Pierre-Renaudel/avenue des Alyscamps (.5 mile [.8 km] southeast from the city center). Tel. 04/90.49.36.87. Open daily May-Sep 9am-7pm, Mar, Apr, and Oct 9am-6pm, Nov-Feb 10:30am-4:30pm. Admission: €5. www.arlestourisme.com.*

Arles Sleeping & Eating
Nord-Pinus €€-€€€

This famous hotel has 27 rooms and an equally famous bar. It's centrally located in historic Arles on the place du Forum. Antiques fill the common areas, and the rooms are interestingly decorated and well-maintained. The hotel is decorated with old bullfighting posters (many bullfighters have stayed here), interesting black-and-white photographs of Africa by Peter Beard, and mosaics. *Info: Place du Forum. Tel. 04/65.88.40.40. V, MC, AE. Bar, AC, TV, telephone. www.nord-pinus.com.*

Hôtel Calendal €€

This is a favorite in Arles. Located near the arena, most of its 38 basic rooms (shower in bathroom, no bathtub) are on a shaded courtyard. Rooms vary in size, so ask to see before you commit. Smaller rooms are much cheaper. Kid-friendly. *Info: 5 rue Porte de Laure. Tel. 04/90.96.11.89. V, MC, AE. AC, TV, hairdryer. www.lecalendal.com.*

The restaurant here, **Le Comptoir du Calendal**, is a pleasant place for a sandwich, snack, and drink when visiting the arena.

Hôtel de l'Amphithéâtre €-€€

This hotel, in a beautifully restored ancient building, is located in the heart of the Old Town near the arena and the ancient theater. A great location for touring the main sights of Arles. Stone steps lead up to the adequate guest rooms. *Info: 5-7 rue Diderot. Tel. 04/90.96.10.30. V, MC, AE. AC, TV, telephone. www.hotelamphitheatre.fr.*

La Gueule du Loup €€-€€€

French and Provençal specialties are served in this small and comfortable restaurant. It's located in a stone building near the arena. Traditional dishes with a contemporary twist. Try the *caillette d'agneau* (lamb baked in Provençal herbs) or the *tartare de thon* (tuna tartare). *Info: 39 rue des Arènes. Tel. 04/90.96.96.69. Closed Wed and Thu. www.restaurant-lagueuleduloup.fr.*

Café Factory République   €-€€
Sit at one of the small tables at this friendly cafe. You can pair your wine or beer with a delicious sandwich or salad or from a selection of straight-forward local dishes. *Info: 35 rue de la République. Tel. 04/90.54.52.23. Closed Sun and Mon.*

The Greenstronome (L'Atelier Jean-Luc Rabanel)   €€€€
Modern Provençal cuisine is featured at this award-winning restaurant. There is no written menu as dishes change based upon what is available from local sources. The restaurant is known for its large wine list. You'll find Asian influences in the chef's innovative dishes. Menus from €95. **Greeniotage** is a few doors down and is overseen by Chef Rabanel. It serves a fixed-price menu for €39. *Info: 7 rue des Carmes. Tel. 04/90.91.07.69. Closed Mon and Tue. Reservations required. www.rabanel.com.*

For those who want luxury accommodations and to dine at the restaurant, there are room and dining packages that begin at €695. There's also a cooking school. Classes from €220. *Reservations through www.rabanel.com.*

Around Arles
St-Rémy-de-Provence
Let's unwind in sophisticated **St-Rémy-de-Provence**. It's 12 miles (19 km) south of Avignon/15 miles (24 km) northeast of Arles. St-Rémy-de-Provence can be reached from Avignon by bus (60 minutes).

Nostradamus, credited with predicting much of the modern era, was born here in 1503. But even he couldn't have foreseen that 500 years later so many would find this the perfect Provence town. Roman ruins are within walking distance of the mansions that grace its historic center. Its most famous resident was Vincent van Gogh, and you can visit the asylum where he spent the last year of his life. But St-Rémy isn't about madness, it's about a calm and sophisticated town where you can experience the best of Provençal life. Boulevards Gambetta, Mirabeau, Marceau, and Victor Hugo circle the town and are lined with cafes and boutiques. Take time to wander the maze of streets in the **Vieille Ville** (Old Town).

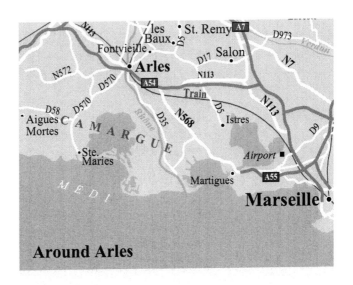

Around Arles

The large church **Collégiale St-Martin** was rebuilt in 1820 (the original church collapsed). Frequent concerts are held featuring its 5,000-pipe organ. *Info: boulevard Marceau. Open daily. Admission: Free.*

St-Rémy-de-Provence Sleeping & Eating
Vallon de Valrugues €€€
Built to look like an Italian villa, this 50-room hotel is set in a park and has all the amenities you could want. Golfers will love its putting green, there are tennis courts, and "foodies" will appreciate the fine cuisine served in the restaurant. *Info: 9 chemin Canto-Cigalo. Tel. 04/90.92.04.40. V, MC, AE. Spa, restaurant, bar, outdoor pool, gym, TV, AC, telephone, minibar, hairdryer, safe. Closed part of Feb. www.vallondevalrugues.com.*

Le Mas des Carassins €€
This farmhouse (*mas*) has been nicely converted into a 14-room hotel complete with pool, restaurant, and mature gardens. *Info: 1 Chemin Gaulois. Tel. 04/90.92.15.48. V, MC, AE. Restaurant, outdoor pool, TV, minibar. www.masdescarassins.com.*

Sous les Figuiers €€

Just a five-minute walk from town, this interesting 14-room boutique hotel is popular with artists. There's a pool, restaurant, and bar. You can relax or paint in the lovely garden under the fig trees. *Info: 3 avenue Gabriel St-Réne Taillandier. Tel. 04/32.60.15.40. V, MC. AC, telephone, safe. www.hotelsouslesfiguiers.com.*

Hôtel du Soleil €€

Just a short walk from the center of town, this hotel is surrounded by gardens, has an outdoor pool, and is decorated in a Provençal theme. Rooms have small, tiled bathrooms. *Info: 35 avenue Pasteur. Tel. 04/90.92.00.63. V, MC, AE. Spa, bar, outdoor pool, TV, AC, telephone, hairdryer, safe. Closed Nov-Feb. www.hotelsoleil.com.*

Les Terrasses de l'Image €€€

Located in the Hôtel de l'Image (€€-€€€), in what once was the town's first hotel, you'll be served contemporary Provençal cuisine. Try the *poulet fermier* (free-range chicken) served in a citrus sauce. This is a lovely place to have a leisurely lunch. There's a restaurant and bistro. *Info: 36 boulevard Victor Hugo. Tel. 04/90.92.51.50. Closed mid-Sep to mid-May. www.hotel-image. fr.* The cocktail bar here is located in a former movie theater. A great place to end your evening, even if you're not dining here.

Bistrot Découverte €€-€€€

This wine bar and bistro is located in the center of St-Rémy. It's known for its list of Provençal wines from small producers. When dining here, try the delicious *la sourie d'agneau de 4 heures, jus à l'ait et au thym* (lamb shank cooked for four hours with a garlic and herb sauce). *Info: 19 boulevard Victor Hugo. Tel. 04/90.92.34.49. Closed Mon.*

St-Rémy-de-Provence Shopping
Fouque

Fascinating collection of antique doors. You can also visit the workshop. *Info: 56 avenue de la Camargue. Tel. 04/90.52.21.90. Workshop: Mon-Fri 8am-noon and 2pm-6pm. Store: Tue-Fri 8am-12:15pm and 2pm-6pm. www.foque.fr.*

A popular and colorful **market** is held Wednesday mornings in and around the place de la République. Great place to find Provençal olive oil.

Joel Durand

Calling all chocoholics! Sample some of the best chocolates in Provence at this small shop. The specialty here is a chocolate with lavender. *Info: 3 boulevard Victor Hugo. Tel. 04/90.92.38.25. Closed Mon. www.joeldurand-chocolatier.fr.*

Glanum

The ancient town of **Glanum** is located on route D5 in the direction of Les Baux (.5 mile [.8 km] south of St-Rémy).

The ruins here date back to the 2nd century BC. You can stroll the streets and building foundations and visit the arch (Arc Municipal) from the time of Julius Caesar. Across the street you'll find Les Antiques, two incredibly well-preserved monuments: the Arc Triomphal (dating from AD 20) and the Mausolée (a mausoleum dating from 30 BC). *Info: On D5 in the direction of Les Baux (.5 mile [.8 km] south of St-Rémy). Tel. 04/90.92.23.79. Open daily Apr-Sep 9:30am-6pm, Oct-Mar 10am-5pm. Closed Mon Oct-Mar. Admission: €8. www.site-glanum.fr.*

The **Monastère de St-Paul-de-Mausole** is near Glanum off route D5 in the direction of Les Baux.

This isolated asylum, a former monastery, still welcomes those in need of help. Its most famous patient, Vincent van Gogh, came here to spend the last year of his life after he allegedly cut off part of his left ear. During his stay, he painted such works as *Olive Trees*. You can tour the columned cloister (with a beautiful garden in the center) and the Romanesque chapel. *Info: Avenue Edgar-le-Roy (near Glanum off D5 in the direction of Les Baux). Tel. 04/90.92.77.00. Open daily Apr-Sep 9:30am-7pm; Oct-Mar 10:15am-noon and 1pm-5:15pm. Admission: €7. www.saintpauldemausole.fr.*

Les Baux-de-Provence

Perched on limestone, **Les Baux-de-Provence** is one of the most dramatic and majestic sights in Provence. It's 11 miles (18 km) northeast of Arles/18 miles (29 km) south of Avignon. Le Baux can be reached from Avignon by bus (65 minutes).

It's hard to distinguish between the buildings and the rocks. The medieval town was home to one of the finest courts in medieval Provence. Abandoned in the 17th century, today it's one of the most visited sights in France. Les Baux gets its name from the mineral bauxite (used in the production of aluminum), which was discovered in the neighboring hills. The village is filled with galleries, boutiques, and cafes operating from the stone houses. On rue Frédéric-Mistral is the Renaissance **Hôtel de Manville**. It's the Town Hall (**Mairie**), and you can visit its courtyard and see changing exhibits. At place St-Vincent you can take in the view, or visit the church **Eglise St-Vincent**, a museum housing works of local artist Yves Brayer, and the small **Chapelle des Pénitents** for a short concert of ancient music.

The main cobbled street is an uphill 15-minute walk. It's hard to describe the clifftop. As you walk among the ruins, you feel like you're in another world. Come here to experience a breathtaking sunset.

The famous **L'Oustau de la Baumanière**, a luxury hotel complex that has been a favorite of everyone from Picasso to Elizabeth Taylor, is also here.

The walls of the ruined citadel of **Château des Baux** date from the 10th century when the first lords settled on this limestone crag. The area below is called the **Val d'Enfer** (Valley of Hell). The **Tour du Brau** still guards the entrance and houses the **Musée d'Histoire des Baux**, filled with models of the town over the ages, medieval weapons, and relics. The small **Chapelle St-Blaise** often shows a short film featuring olive orchards painted by van Gogh, Gauguin, and Cézanne. On weekends from April through September, the castle presents medieval pageants. *Info: Tel. 04/90.49.20.02. Open daily Apr-Jun and Sep 9am-7pm, Jul and Aug 9am-7:30pm, Jan-Feb and Nov-Dec 10am-5pm, Mar and Oct 9:30am-6:30pm. Admission: €10. www.chateau-baux-provence.com.*

Carrière des Lumières

You can watch a state-of-the-art, 40-minute slide show in a former quarry, where 50 projectors flash images on the limestone walls. It's mesmerizing. There's a new program each year. *Info: Val d'Enfer (Valley of Hell). Below Les Baux on route D27. Tel. 04/90.54.38.65. Open daily Jan, Nov, and Dec 10am-6pm; Feb-Mar 9:30am-6pm; Apr-Jun and Sep-Oct 9:30am-7pm; Jul and Aug 9am-7:30pm. Closed Feb. Admission: €14.50. www.carrieres-lumieres.com.*

Les-Baux-de-Provence Sleeping & Eating
Auberge de la Benvengudo €€-€€€

A country house that's been lovingly converted to a charming hotel one mile (1.6 km) south of Les Baux. Surrounded by gardens, the rooms and apartments are each beautifully decorated with antique furniture. All rooms have either a patio or balcony. The smaller rooms are a better deal. Beautiful outdoor pool. *Info: Vallon de l'Arcoule (on D78, the route to Arles). Tel. 04/90.54.32.54. V, MC, AE. Restaurant (see below), outdoor pool, tennis courts, AC, TV, telephone. Closed Nov-Feb. www.benvengudo.com.*

Auberge de la Benvengudo €€€

Authentic Provençal cuisine, such as *gigot d'Agneau aux pigons* (leg of lamb with pine nuts) served at this lovely country house and inn located one mile (1.6 km) south of Les Baux. There's an impressive list of regional wines. Fixed three-course menu €78. *Info: Vallon de l'Arcoule (on D78, the route to Arles). Tel. 04/90.54.32.54. Reservations required. Open Mar-Oct. www.benvengudo.com.*

La Reine Jeanne €€-€€€

This small inn at the entrance to the village has an attractive terrace and dining room. Stop in for panoramic views, especially at sunset, and straight-forward cooking. Try the *magret de canard* (duck breast) *Info: 4 rue Porte Mages. Tel. 04/90.54.32.06. Open daily. www.la-reinejeanne.fr.*

The Camargue

The Camargue–the land of French cowboys–is nine miles (15 km) south of Arles on route D570/12 miles (19 km) east of Aigues-Mortes.

This huge (309 square miles [497 km]) area is a wetlands delta where the Rhône River breaks in two before spilling into the Mediterranean Sea. It's mostly swamp, and mosquitoes are bothersome. The only people who seem to be able to tolerate the conditions are *gardiens*, cowboys who ride white horses and raise bulls here. Part of The Camargue is filled with rice fields, cattle ranches, and stud farms. The other part is a national park (**Parc Regional de Camargue**). It's home to thousands of flamingos, and is a bird-lovers paradise. The **Parc Ornithologique du Pont de Gau** is a protected area for over 400 species of birds. You can spend an entire day here exploring this national park, away from all the other tourists.

Stes-Maries-de-la-Mer

Stes-Maries-de-la-Mer is 24 miles (39 km) south of Arles/10 miles (18 km) south of the Camargue/80 miles (129 km) west of Marseille.

According to legend, Mary Magdalene, Mary Salome, and Mary Jacobé left ancient Israel and landed in a boat here. Depending on which version you believe, they either arrived with, or were greeted and helped by, Sara, a gypsy. The town, which has a whitewashed Spanish flavor to it, is a budget beach resort and very touristy. In May and October, it's loaded with Romani who come to the town's church as part of a pilgrimage to honor Sara.

You can't miss the church **Eglise des Stes-Maries** with its large bell tower (*see photo on preceding page*). The dark interior is filled with notes of thanks to the three Saint Marys. Note the carved boat with statues of Mary Magdalene and the Virgin Mary. The observation area has views of the town, its beaches and the Camargue.

There are plenty of casual and inexpensive eateries. There are also many places to ride the famous white horses that are raised here on route D570 as you enter town.

Aigues-Mortes

Not too far from Stes-Maries-de-la-Mer is another touristy, but peculiar, town. **Aigues-Mortes** is 11 miles (19 km) northwest of Stes-Maries-de-la-Mer/29 miles (48 km) southwest of Arles/25 miles (41 km) south of Nîmes.

France's best-preserved walled town, Aigues-Mortes means "dead waters," an appropriate name, as it's surrounded by swamp. *See photo below.* It was once a port town and departure point for Louis IX and his crusaders bound for the Holy Land. Inside the fortress walls is a small village.

Among the many souvenir shops is the stark church **Eglise Notre-Dame des Sablons** and the attractive place St-Louis dominated by a statue of Louis IX. The **Tour de Constance** is a tower (complete with elevator) that affords views of The Camargue.

8. MARSEILLE

HIGHLIGHTS
- The Old Port and museums in Marseille
- Sunbathing on the beach in Cassis and Bandol
- The fjord-like Calanques
- Les Gorges du Verdon

Cosmopolitan and diverse Marseille, the breathtaking Grand Canyon du Verdun, vineyards, and seafront resorts offer the traveler a little bit of everything in this area of Provence.

Marseille was founded over 2,600 years ago, making it France's oldest city. It's also the second largest city in the country. Many travelers, put off by its urban sprawl, avoid it, as most come to this part of the country for quiet villages. Those who do choose to spend time here will be rewarded, as Marseille is a vibrant and cosmopolitan city. Marseille was designated the European Capital of Culture for 2013. As a result, new museums have opened, older museums have been renovated, and many neighborhoods have been transformed.

Marseille (population 900,000) is in the south of France on the Mediterranean Sea. It's 411 miles (662 km) south of Paris and 117 miles (188 km) west of Nice. The **Marseille Airport** (located in Marignane) is 17 miles (27 km) northwest of the city. Minivans (called *navettes*) leave for Marseille's St-Charles rail station every 15 minutes for €10. Bus and metro tickets are €2 single ride and €5.20 for a day pass.

Sights
Vieux Port (Old Port)
Industrial shipping has moved away from the Old Port, and now mostly pleasure boats are docked here. If arriving by car, follow the signs to Centre-Ville and Vieux Port. From the train station, Gare St-Charles, it's a 15-minute downhill walk to the port. It's dominated by two forts (**Fort St-Jean** and **Fort St-Nicolas**), and is the heart of the city. You'll find a huge fish market here every day until early afternoon.

Bouillabaisse
Don't leave Marseille without trying its world-renowned *bouillabaisse*. There are two main varieties: *bouillabaisse du pêcheur* (with three types of fish) and *bouillabaisse du ravi* (with six different types of fish). Delicious! **Miramar**, on the Old Port, is known for this specialty (12 quai du Port). *lemiramar.fr.*

Marseille
1. Abbaye St-Victor
2. Cathédrale de la Nouvelle Major
3. Centre de la Vieille Charité
4. Fort St-Jean
5. Fort St-Nicolas
6. Hôtel de Ville (City Hall)
7. La Canebière
8. Le Panier (Old Town)
9. Musée Cantini
10. MuCEM
11. Musée d'Histoire de Marseille
12. Musée Regards de Provence
13. Palais Longchamp
14. Villa Méditerranée/Cosquer
     Méditerranée

M Metro Stop
P Parking

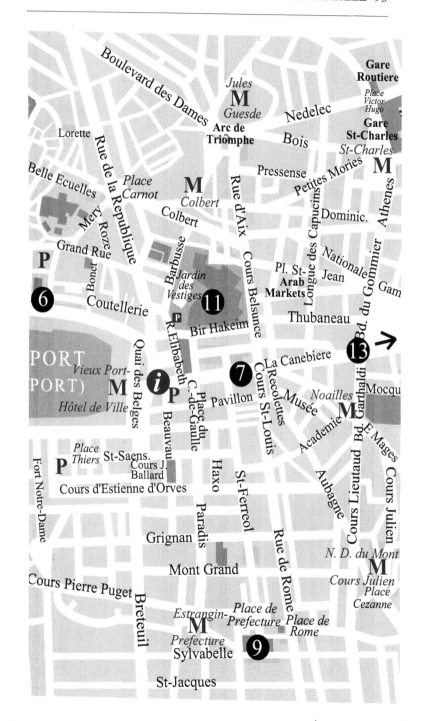

On the port is the ornate **Hôtel de Ville** (City Hall). If you walk uphill from City Hall, you'll be in **Le Panier** (Old Town), the oldest section of Marseille. Wander the tiny squares, cobblestone streets, and stone stairways. Thankfully, after years of neglect, the Old Town is coming back to life.

At the top of Le Panier is the **Centre de la Vieille Charité** (Center of the Old Charity). This spectacular 17th-century building (a former poorhouse) houses two museums: the **Musée d'Arts Africains, Océaniens, et Amérindiens** (Museum of African, Oceanic and American Indian Art) and the **Musée d'Archéologie Mediterranéenne** (Museum of Mediterranean Archeology). *Info: 2 rue de la Charité (at the top of the Old Town). Tel. 04/91.14.58.80. Open Tue-Sun 10am-6pm. Closed Mon. Admission: €6. vieille-charite-marseille.com.*

Also here is the **Cathédrale de la Nouvelle Major.** This huge 19th-century cathedral, located in the Old Town, is neo-Byzantine (lots of marble). *Info: Place de la Major (in the Old Town). Open daily. Admission: Free.*

Ferries depart from quai des Belges to **Château d'If.** This offshore island fortress was long used as a prison, and was made famous in *The Count of Monte Cristo. Info: Open Apr-Sep 10am-6pm, Oct-Mar 10:30am-5:15pm. Closed Mon Oct-Mar. Admission: €6. Ferry ride from the port to island: From €11. www.chateau-if.fr.*

If you're interested in shopping, head to **La Canebière.** Marseille's main boulevard begins at the Old Port and stretches through the center of the city, and it's loaded with cafes, shops of all sorts, sailors, and people of every imaginable nationality.

At the **Musée d'Histoire de Marseille/Jardin des Vestiges** (Marseille History Museum/Garden of Remains), you can view current archeological excavations in the garden, and visit the museum to see archeological finds from France's oldest city. A highlight is the 3rd-century merchant vessel discovered in the Old Port. *Info: 2 rue Henri-Barbusse. Tel. 04/91.55.36.63. Open Tue-Sun 9:30am-6pm. Closed Mon. Admission: €6. www.musee-histoire-marseille-voie-historique.fr.*

 If you keep walking up La Canebière, you'll run into the **Palais Longchamp**. Built during the Second Empire, this spectacular palace won't disappoint with fountains, sculptures, and columns. Both the fine-arts and natural-history museums are located here. *Info: place Bernex. Tel. 04/91.14.59.30. Open Tue-Sun 9am-6pm. Closed Mon. Admis-*

On the other side of the Old Port from La Panier (Old Town) are two other sights you can see if you have the time. The basilica **Abbaye St-Victor** sits above a 5th-century crypt said to contain the remains of the martyr St. Cassianus. *Info: Place St-Victor. Tel. 04/96.11.22.60. Open daily 9am-7pm. Admission: Free. €2 to the crypt.*

The **Musée Cantini** is a modern art museum featuring exhibits of some of the world's up-and-coming artists. The museum's permanent collection has a large collection of Surrealist art. Some of the artists featured here are Kandinsky, Dubuffet, Bacon, Signac, Léger, and Ernst. *Info: 19 rue Grignan. Tel. 04/13.94.83.30. Open Tue-Sun 9am-6pm. Closed Mon. Admission: Permanent collection is free.*

Notre-Dame de la Garde is topped by a gold statue of the Virgin Mary. This gigantic Romanesque-Byzantine basilica is 500 feet above the harbor. The elegant interior is filled with marble and mosaics, and the views outside are spectacular. *Info: rue Fort-du-Sanctuaire (30-minute walk from harbor). Tel. 04/91.13.40.80. Open daily 7am-6pm. Admission: Free. www.notredamedelagarde.fr.*

Marseille has several new museums located near Fort-St-Jean in the Old Port:

MuCEM (Musée des Civilisations de L'Europe et de la Mediterranée): The Museum of European and Mediterranean Civilizations houses a collection of 250,000 art and artifacts from areas around the Mediterranean. The contemporary building is

encased in an interesting concrete "lace" and connected to the Fort St-Jean by a spectacular elevated walkway. *Info: Quai du Port. Tel. 04/84.35.13.13. Open Wed-Mon 10am-8pm in summer (until 6pm in winter). Closed Tue. Admission: €11.* *www.mucem.org.*

Villa Méditerranée: This center, next to MuCEM, host exhibits, performances, and concerts all with the theme of bringing together Mediterranean cultures. The modern building features a huge cantilevered overhang above a reflecting pool. The entire lower floor is below sea level. *Info: Esplanade de J4. Tel. 04/95.09.42.70. Open Tue-Fri noon-6pm, Sat and Sun 10am-6pm. Closed Mon. Admission: Depends on the exhibit.*

Musée Regards de Provence: Located near MuCEM and Villa Méditerranée, this new museum features Provençal and Mediterranean art and media from the 18th to the 21st centuries. The real attraction here is the rooftop restaurant with incredible views of the nearby Cathédrale de la Nouvelle Major. It's hard to believe that this building was once the station where immigrants were disinfected prior to entry to France. *Info: rue Voudoyer. Tel. 04/96.17.40.40. Open Tue-Sun 10am-6pm. Closed Mon. Admission: €7.50. www.museeregardsdeprovence.com.*

Cosquer Méditerranée: This new interactive museum recreates the Grotte Cosquer, an underwater cave with prehistoric paintings, discovered in 1985 off the coast near Marseille. An elevator plunges you "underwater," to the basement of the museum, where you'll take a ride through the cave. *Info: Promenade Robert Laffont. Tel. 04/91/31/23/12. Open daily 10am-6:30pm (Jul and Aug 9am-9pm). Admission: €11. www.grotte-cosquer.com.*

Markets

Marseille has a large Tunisian, Algerian, and Moroccan population. You'll feel as if you are in North Africa at one of the city's large **Arab Markets**. The largest is found off La Canebière on rue Longue des Capucins. Don't miss it! There's a huge **fish market** at the Old Port on quai des Belges every day until early afternoon.

Marseille Sleeping & Eating
Sofitel Marseille (Vieux Port) €€€

This 133-room contemporary hotel above the old port offers modern conveniences and is popular with business travelers. Good location for seeing the port's major sights. *Info: 36 boulevard Charles-Livon. Tel. 04/91.15.59.00. V, MC, AE. Restaurant, bar, AC, TV, telephone, minibar, in-room safe, hairdryer. www.sofitel-marseille-vieuxport.com.*

The 110-room **Novotel (Vieux Port)** is in the same building, and shares some staff. This less expensive (€€) cousin has smaller rooms and fewer amenities, but is still a good choice. *Info: 36 boulevard Charles-Livon. Tel. 04/96.11.42.11. V, MC, AE. Restaurant, bar, AC, TV, telephone, minibar, hairdryer. www.accor.com.*

Les Arcenaulx €€€

Provençal cuisine with outdoor dining near the Old Port. When available, try the *fleurs de courgette et gorgonzola* (zucchini flowers with gorgonzola). You can visit the connected bookstore after your meal. *Info: 25 cours d'Estienne d'Orves. Tel. 04/91.59.80.30. Closed Sun. www.les-arcenaulx.com.*

Chez Ida €€

Packed, popular, and fun. This restaurant is centrally located near place Jean Jaurès. Try the baked sea bass and the gazpacho. To add to the fun, they have karaoke some evenings. *Info: 7 rue Ferdinand Rey. Tel. 04/91.47.04.97. Lunch Mon-Fri. Dinner Fri and Sat. Closed Sun. www.chezida.fr.*

Bar de la Marine €€

On the Old Port, this bar is popular with locals for lunch. *Info: 15 quai de Rive-Neuve. Tel. 04/91.54.95.42. Open daily.*

Cassis, Bandol, & The Calanques

The coast of Provence offers you the choice of two relaxing port towns. First, we'll head to **Cassis**. It's 19 miles (30 km) east of Marseille/25 miles (42 km) west of Toulon.

Waterfront cafes around a beautiful port, buildings painted in pastels, boutiques, and a medieval castle (the **Château de Cassis**) all make this Provence's most attractive coastal town. *See photo on page 100.* The water is clean and clear, and the beaches, like many others on this coast, are pebbly rather than sandy. The 1,200-foot cliff above the *château* is **Cap Canaille**, Europe's highest coastal cliff. Frankly, there isn't much to do in Cassis except lie on the beach and either look at the castle or the beachgoers, but, after all, that's what you came here for. Parking is scarce in town, so you can park outside and take a shuttle bus into town (watch for the signs saying "navette"). They depart every 15 minutes (€1.60).

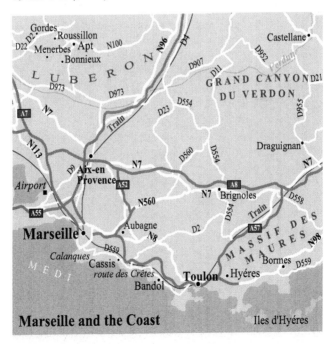

Marseille and the Coast

Don't forget to try the aromatic white wines that are produced in the hills surrounding Cassis. There are several vineyards outside of town that offer wine tastings. One is **Domaine Ferme Blanc** on route D559, *Tel. 04/42.01.00.74.* *www.domainedelafermeblanche.com.*

Between Cassis and Bandol are the **Calanques**. Like fjords, these cliffs border the coast and hide beautiful beaches with clear blue water. You can either take a boat or hiking tour (several companies operate from the harbor in Cassis with tour prices beginning at €19, *www.ot-cassis.com*) to explore the three calanques: **Calanque En Vau**, **Calanque Port Pin**, and **Calanque Port Miou**. If you're not interested in hiking or the boat tour, the **route des Crêtes**, which heads east out of town following the signs for La Ciotat/Toulon, provides spectacular views of the coast. Note that this road is not for nervous drivers. It's very scary at points, with no guardrails protecting you from plunging straight down the cliff!

Bandol is 15 miles (24 km) southeast of Cassis/nine miles (15 km) west of Toulon. On the western end of the Côte d'Azur, this popular seaside resort town is best known for its beaches, seaside casino, yacht-filled harbor, and waterfront promenade lined with palm trees. There are 25 hotels here, and even more eating establishments. Most know the town for the wine that carries its name. The red is full-bodied and spicy, while the white is fruity, often with a hint of aniseed.

Cassis Sleeping & Eating
Hôtel de la Plage Mahogany €€-€€€
This 30-room hotel faces the Mediterranean and the coastal cliff. Nineteen of the rooms have balconies with sea views where you can enjoy breakfast which is included in the price (and later a glass of Cassis wine). Fantastic location for a short walk into town to dine or to the beach. The friendly staff is ready to help you with reservations for dinner or local activities. *Info: Plage du Bestouan. Tel. 04/42.01.05.70. V, MC. Beach restaurant, AC (in most rooms), TV, telephone, minibar, hairdryer.*
www.hotelmahogany.com.

During the summer, the hotel restaurant **"La Calanque M"** is open every evening and Sunday for lunch (€€€). The emphasis is on seafood, but you can also try the delicious *côte de veau au citron* (veal chop served in a citrus sauce). *Info: Tel. 04/42.01.05.70. Open Thu-Mon for dinner, Sat and Sun for lunch and dinner. Closed Tue and Wed.*

Hôtel Royal Cottage €€
This 25-room hotel is located on the hillside only a five-minute walk to the port (it's a steep walk back). Comfortable and clean rooms, helpful staff, and a delightful outdoor swimming pool surrounded by palm trees where you can have a light lunch in the summer. *Info: 6 avenue du 11 Novembre. Tel. 04/42.01.33.34. V, MC. Outdoor pool, AC, TV, telephone, minibar, in-room safe, hairdryer. www.royal-cottage.com.*

Hôtel de France Maguy/Hotel Eden Cassis €-€€

Located a few blocks from the port, this 10-room hotel has small, clean rooms. The more expensive rooms have little patios or balconies. There is secure, private parking. *Info: Avenue du Revestel. Tel. 04/42.01.72.21. V, MC, AE. Pool, AC, TV, telephone, hairdryer. www.www.hoteldefrancemaguy.com.*

Le Bistrot de Nino €€-€€€

Grilled fish, *bouillabaisse,* and sea urchins (a local specialty) are what to expect at this harborside restaurant. *Info: Quai Barthélémy (on the harbor). Tel. 04/42.36.94.09.*

Le Chaudron €€-€€€

This bistro is located on one of the backstreets of Cassis and not too far the port. It's family-run and friendly. Provençal cuisine with an emphasis on fresh seafood. Whatever you eat, make sure you order one of the local Cassis wines available here! *Info: 4 rue Adolphe Thiers. Tel. 04/42.01.74.18. open Mar-Dec. Closed Tue.*

La Villa Madie €€€€

Refined Mediterranean cuisine, featuring fresh fish and local produce, is served at this restaurant sitting on a cliff above the bay. The views from the terrace are incredible. The **Brasserie du Corton** (€€-€€€) serves equally inventive dishes for lunch Mon-Fri. *Info: Avenue de Revestel, Anse de Corton. Tel. 04/96.18.00.00. Closed Mon-Wed. www.lavillamadie.com.*

Massif des Maures

The **Massif des Maures** is between route N98 (the coastal road) and route A8. North from route N98 is the mountainous route D14. Hope you like hairpin turns!

It's hard to believe that this hilly, thickly wooded and sparsely populated area is so close to the frenetic coastal resorts of the western Riviera. The Massif des Maures stretches from Hyères to Fréjus, and much of it's inaccessible. The hills are by no means huge, but the sudden drops in the winding roads and the views make this an interesting detour from the touristy coast.

There's a footpath called the GR9 for experienced hikers. "GR" stands for Grandes Randonnées, national hiking trails. It follows the highest ridge of the Massif des Maures.

Les Gorges du Verdon

The Grand Canyon of Verdon–**Les Gorges du Verdon**–can be visited by traveling along two cliffside roads stretching from Moustiers-Ste-Marie to Castellane. **La Corniche Sublime** (routes D19 to D71) is along the southern rim including **Pont de l'Artuby**, the highest bridge in Europe. **La route des Crêtes** (routes D952 and D23) follows the northern rim including **Point Sublime**, the viewpoint at the entrance to the canyon. From here, the adventurous GR4 trail leads you to the bottom of the canyon, which can be reached only by foot or raft.

Hello, Gorgeous! The green waters of the Verdun River have sliced through limestone and created one of the great natural sights of not only Provence, but of France and all of Europe. This canyon is 13 miles (21 km) long and as deep as 2,300 feet (701 meters). At points, it's only 26 feet (8 meters) wide.

The huge area around the canyon is a nature-lover's smorgasbord of pristine lakes, trickling streams, alpine scenery, and picture-postcard villages such as **Aiguines** and **Moustiers-Ste-Marie**. A drive around the canyon can take up to three hours and even longer in the summer. You'll need to fill your tank before you get to the canyon. Expect hairpin turns, along with fantastic scenery. There are many areas to stop and walk or just take in the breath-taking vistas.

9. PLANNING YOUR TRIP

GETTING TO PROVENCE
Airport/Arrival
The Marseille Airport (located in Marignane) is 17 miles north-west of the city. Minivans (called *navettes*) leave for Marseille's St-Charles rail station every 15 minutes for €10. Bus and metro tickets are €2 single ride and €5.20 for a day pass.

The **Nice-Côte d'Azur Airport** is on a peninsula 20 minutes west of the central city of Nice. A taxi into town costs between €35-€40. Rideshare to central Nice costs around €25.

You can hop on the convenient Tram 2 at the baggage claim exit. It takes you to the Jean Médecin station in the heart of Nice. The average journey time is 30 minutes. This tram line ends at Port Lympia. Trams run every day, except May 1, from 5am until midnight.

For €1.50, a single pass has unlimited transfers on buses or trams within 74 minutes of validation (one direction only). Bus tickets may be purchased from the driver, but tram tickets must be purchased before boarding at vending machines at the stop. The machines only take credit cards with chips or euro coins. A 10-ride pass is €10 (€1 per ride).

All major car rental companies are represented at both airports.

GETTING AROUND
Cars & Driving
Renting a car and driving is the best way to see the areas covered in this book. Note that parking can be difficult in high season. Driving within major cities can be a headache. Gas is very expensive, but a mitigating factor is that the cars are smaller and more energy-efficient. You will either take a ticket when you get on the autoroute and pay (look for the signs that say *péage*) when you get off, or pay as you go. One kilometer = 0.62 miles. To convert miles to kilometers, multiply by 1.61. So, 1 mile = 1.61 kilometers.

In order of fastest to slowest, routes are as follows: A means autoroute, N means national route, and D means departmental route. Be prepared for narrow roads, high speeds, and hairpin turns.

Train & Bus Travel

SNCF is the rail system for France. TGV trains are fast-speed trains that travel an average of 279 mph (449 kph). TGV trains departing from Paris's Charles-de-Gaulle Airport serve Aix-en-Provence (3 hours), Arles (4 hours), Avignon (2 hours and 40 minutes), Cannes (6 hours via Marseille), Nîmes (3 hours), Marseille (3 hours and 15 minutes), and Orange (3 hours). Aix-en-Provence and Avignon have TGV stations on the edge of town. The trip on the TGV from Paris to Nice is 6 hours, as not all of the trip is high-speed. *Info: www.sncf.com.*

There's a coastal rail line that runs from Ventimiglia on the Italian border (Vintimille in French) to Marseille. There are trains that run nearly every hour on this line. Stops on this scenic train ride include: Menton, Cap-Martin, Monaco, Èze-sur-Mer (not to be confused with hilltop Èze), Beaulieu, St-Jean-Cap-Ferrat, Villefranche-sur-Mer, Nice, Antibes, and Cannes. You must validate (*composter*) your ticket at a machine (watch locals do it) before you get on a SNCF train.

Regional bus service is good, but is limited on Sundays. Train service is in most cases faster, but bus service is generally cheaper.

BASIC INFORMATION
Banking & Changing Money

The **euro** (**€**) is the currency of France and most of Europe. Before you leave, it's a good idea to get some euros. It makes your arrival a lot easier. ATMs at the airport are also available to get euros on your arrival. Call your credit card company or bank before you leave to tell them that you'll be using your ATM or credit card outside the country. Many have automatic controls that can "freeze" your account if the computer program determines that there are charges outside your normal area. ATMs (of course, with fees) are the easiest way to change money in France. You'll find them everywhere. Most places no longer accept traveler's checks due to counterfeit checks.

Business Hours

Many attractions and offices in Provence close at noon and re-open and hour or two later.

Climate & Weather

Expect hot and dry weather except for periods of heavy rain in spring. November, December, and January can be quite cold and wet, with temperatures dipping to lows in the 30s (-1C). The average high temperature in July and August is 84 degrees (29C). The Mistral wind blows 30 to 60 miles per hour (48-96 kph) about 100 days of the year in Provence. It begins above the Alps and Massif Central Mountains, gaining speed as it heads south toward the Mediterranean Sea. Le Mistral is followed by clear skies. France uses Celsius to record temperatures. Check *www. weather.com* before you leave.

Consulates & Embassies

• US Consulate, Marseille: place Varian Fry, Tel. 01/43.12.48.85.
• Canadian Consulate, Nice: 37 boulevard Dubouchage, Tel. 04/93.13.17.19.
• UK Consulate, Marseille: 10 place de la Joliette, Tel. 04/91.15.72.10.

Holidays

• New Year's: January 1
• Easter
• Ascension (40 days after Easter)
• Pentecost (seventh Sunday after Easter)
• May Day: May 1
• Victory in Europe: May 8
• Bastille Day: July 14
• Assumption of the Virgin Mary: August 15
• All Saints': November 1
• Armistice: November 11
• Christmas: December 25

Electricity

The electrical current in Paris is 220 volts as opposed to 110 volts found at home. Don't fry your electric razor, hairdryer, or laptop. You'll need a converter and an adapter. (Most laptops don't require a converter, but why are you bringing that anyway?)

Emergencies & Safety

Don't wear a fanny pack; it's a sign that you're a tourist and an easy target (especially in crowded tourist areas). Avoid wearing expensive jewelry. Don't leave valuables in your car. In case of an emergency, dial 112. Pharmacies can refer you to a doctor.

Insurance

Check with your health-care provider. Most policies don't cover you overseas. If that's the case, you may want to obtain medical insurance. Given the uncertainties in today's world, you may also want to purchase trip-cancellation insurance (for insurance coverage, check out *www.insuremytrip.com*). Make sure that your policy covers sickness, disasters, bankruptcy, and State Department travel restrictions and warnings. In other words, read the fine print!

Internet Access

Wi-Fi is available at most bars, cafes, and restaurants.

Language

Please, make the effort to speak a little French. It will get you a long way—even if all you can say is *Parlez-vous anglais?* (par-lay voo ahn-glay): Do you speak English? Gone are the days when the French were only interested in correcting your French.

You'll find helpful French phrases a few pages below.

Packing

Never pack prescription drugs, eyeglasses, or valuables. Carry them on. Think black. It always works for men and women. Oh, and by the way, pack light. Don't ruin your trip by having to lug around huge suitcases.

Before you leave home, make copies of your passport, airline tickets, and confirmation of hotel reservations. You should also make a list of your credit card numbers and the telephone numbers for your credit card companies. If you lose any of them (or they're stolen), you can call someone at home and have them provide the information to you. You should also pack copies of these documents separate from the originals.

Passport Regulations

You'll need a valid passport to enter France. If you're staying for more than 90 days, you must obtain a visa. US citizens who have been away over 48 hours can bring home $800 of merchandise duty-free every 30 days. *Info: help.cbp.gov.* Canadians don't need visas. Canadians can bring back C$750 each year if they have been gone for 7 days or more. *travel.gc.ca.*

Hotel and restaurant prices are required by law to include taxes and service charges. **Value Added Tax** (VAT, or TVA in France) is nearly 20% (higher on luxury goods). The VAT is included in the price of goods (except services such as restaurants). Foreigners are entitled to a refund but must fill out a refund form. When you make your purchase, ask for the form and instructions if you're purchasing €175 or more in one place and in one day (no combining). It can be a hassle. Check out *www.global-blue.com* for the latest information on refunds (and help for a fee).

Postal Services

Post offices–PTT–are found in nearly every town. You'll recognize them by their yellow La Poste signs. They're generally open weekdays from 8am-7pm and Saturdays from 8am until noon. Some post offices, especially those in smaller towns, close for an hour or two in the middle of the day.

Rest Rooms

There aren't a lot of public restrooms. If you need to go, your best bet is to head (no pun intended) to the nearest cafe or brasserie. It's considered good manners to purchase something if you use the restroom. Don't be shocked to walk into a restroom and find two porcelain foot prints and a hole in the floor. A few of these old "squat toilets" still exist. Hope you have strong thighs!

Telephone
• Country code for France is 33
• Area code for Provence and the French Riviera is 04
• Calls beginning with 0800 are toll-free
• Calling France from the U.S. and Canada: dial 011-33-4 plus the eight-digit local number. You drop the 0 in the area code

• Calling the U.S. or Canada from Paris: dial 00 (wait for the tone), dial 1 plus the area code and local number
• Calling within Provence and the French Riviera: dial 04 and the eight-digit local number.
• The prefixes 06 and 07 are reserved for cell phones.

Phone cards are the cheapest way to call. Get one from many *tabacs* or magazine kiosks. A great way to stay in touch and save money is to rent an international cell phone. One provider is *www.cellhire.com*. If you're a frequent visitor to Europe, you may want to purchase a cell phone (for about $50) from *www.mobal. com*. You'll get an international telephone number and pay by the minute for calls made. If you are using a smartphone, make sure to turn off your international roaming (and use Wi-Fi instead) to save money. You can purchase an international prepaid SIM card at *www.simoptions.com*.

Time
When it's noon in New York City, it's 6pm in Provence. For hours of events or schedules, the French use the 24-hour clock. So 6am is 06h00 and 1pm is 13h00.

Tipping
See the Restaurants section, beginning on page 110, for tipping in restaurants. Other tips: up to 5% for taxi drivers, €1 for room service, €1.50 per bag to the hotel porter, €1.50 per day for maid service and €0.50 to bathroom attendants.

Tourist Information
Nearly every town in this book has a helpful tourist-information center.

Water
Tap water is safe in France. Occasionally, you'll find *non potable* signs in rest rooms. This means that the water is not safe for drinking.

Web Sites
For the French Government Tourist Office *www.franceguide.com*. US State Department Foreign Entry Requirements *www.state.gov*. Made Easy Travel Guides *www.madeeasytravelguides.com*.

Hotels & Restaurants
Hotels

We've listed hotels throughout Provence in this book. We've also included some wonderful bed-and-breakfast establishments and farmhouses that have been converted into inns and hotels.

Hotel Prices in this Book
Prices for two people in a double room:

- Expensive (over €200): €€€
- Moderate (€100-200): €€
- Inexpensive (under €100): €

In addition to the lodgings in this book, you could also stay at one of the many *gîtes* (country homes that can be rented by travelers, usually by the week). In an effort to preserve these country homes, the French government offers subsidies to rehabilitate them and a program to market them for rental. There are thousands of these homes in France, from luxury to budget. For information on this great way to experience France, especially if traveling as a family or group, visit *www.gites.com*.

Restaurants

You've come to France in part to enjoy the best cuisine in the world, right? You will not be disappointed. We have selected the best restaurants within different price ranges, and we also give you some tips to help you save money and still eat a meal that will be memorable and fantastic in every way!

There's no need to spend a lot of money in Provence to eat well. There are all kinds of fabulous foods to be had inexpensively.

Eat at a neighborhood restaurant or bistro. You'll always know the price of a meal before entering, as almost all restaurants post the menu and prices in the window. Never order anything whose price is not known in advance. If you see *selon grosseur* (sometimes abbreviated as s/g) this means that you're paying by weight, which can be extremely expensive.

Restaurant Prices in this Book
Restaurant prices in this book are for a main course.

- Expensive: (over €20) €€€
- Moderate: (€10-20) €€
- Inexpensive: (under €10) €

Delis and food stores can provide cheap and wonderful meals. Buy some cheese, bread, wine, and other snacks and have a picnic. In fact, no matter what, you should go into a *boulangerie* and buy a baguette at least once.

Lunch, even at the most expensive restaurants listed in this guide, always has a lower fixed price. So have lunch as your main meal. Many French do.

Restaurants and bistros that have menus written in English (especially those near tourist attractions) are almost always more expensive than neighborhood restaurants and bistros.

Street vendors in larger towns generally sell inexpensive and terrific food; you'll find excellent hot dogs, *crêpes,* and roast-chicken sandwiches.

For the cost of a cup of coffee or a drink, you can linger at a cafe and watch the world pass you by for as long as you want. It's one of France's greatest bargains.

The bill in a restaurant is called *l'addition* ... but the bill in a bar is called *le compte* or *la note.* Confused? It's easier if you just make a scribbling motion with your fingers on the palm of your hand.

Tipping
A service charge is almost always added to your bill. Depending on the service, it's *sometimes* appropriate to leave up to 5%. Most locals round up to the next euro and it's okay if that is what you do, too. Travelers from the U.S. sometimes have trouble *not* tipping. Remember, you do not have to tip.

The menu will usually note that service is included (*service compris*). Sometimes this is abbreviated with the letters s.c. The letters s.n.c. stand for *service non compris*; this means that the service is not included in the price, and you must leave a tip. This is *extremely* rare. You'll sometimes find *couvert* or cover charge on your menu (a small charge just for placing your butt at the table).

Menu

A menu is a fixed-price meal, not that piece of paper listing the food items. If you want what we consider a menu, you need to ask for *la carte*. The menu is almost always posted on the front of the restaurant so you know what you're getting into, both foodwise and pricewise, before you enter.

Mealtimes

Lunch is served from around 1pm and dinner from around 8pm. Make reservations!

Dogs Allowed!

The French really love their dogs. In restaurants, it's not uncommon to find several dogs under tables, or even on their own chairs.

ESSENTIAL FRENCH PHRASES

please, *s'il vous plaît* (seel voo *play*)
thank you, *merci* (*mair* see)
yes, *oui* (wee)
no, *non* (nohn)
good morning, *bonjour* (bohn *jhoor*)
good afternoon, *bonjour* (bohn *jhoor*)
good evening, *bonsoir* (bohn *swahr*)
goodbye, *au revoir* (o ruh *vwahr*)
sorry/excuse me, *pardon* (pahr-*dohn*)
you are welcome, *de rien* (duh ree *ehn*)

do you speak English?, *parlez-vous anglais?* (par lay voo ahn *glay*)
I don't speak French, *je ne parle pas français* (jhuh ne parl pah frahn *say*)
I don't understand, *je ne comprends pas* (jhuh ne kohm *prahn* pas)
I'd like a table, *je voudrais une table* (zhuh voo *dray* ewn tabl)
I'd like to reserve a table, *je voudrais réserver une table* (zhuh voo *dray* rayzehrvay ewn tabl)
for one, *pour un* (poor oon), *deux* (duh)(2), *trois* (twah)(3), *quatre* (*kaht*-ruh)(4), *cinq* (sank)(5), *six* (cease)(6), *sept* (set)(7), *huit* (wheat)(8), *neuf* (nerf)(9), *dix* (dease)(10)
waiter/sir, *monsieur* (muh-*syuh*) (never *garçon!*)
waitress/miss, *mademoiselle* (mad mwa *zel*)
knife, *couteau* (koo *toe*)
spoon, *cuillère* (kwee *air*)
fork, *fourchette* (four *shet*)
menu, *la carte* (la cart) (not *menu!*)
wine list, *la carte des vins* (la cart day van)
no smoking, *défense de fumer* (day *fahns* de fu may)
toilets, *les toilettes* (lay twa *lets*)

closed, *fermé* (fehr-may)
open, *ouvert* (oo-vehr)
today, *aujourd'hui* (o zhoor *dwee*)
tomorrow, *demain* (duh *mehn*)
tonight, *ce soir* (suh *swahr*)

Monday, *lundi* (luhn *dee*)
Tuesday, *mardi* (mahr *dee*)
Wednesday, *mercredi* (mair kruh *dee*)
Thursday, *jeudi* (jheu *dee*)
Friday, *vendredi* (vawn druh *dee*)
Saturday, *samedi* (sahm *dee*)
Sunday, *dimanche* (dee *mahnsh*)

here, *ici* (ee-*see*)
there, *là* (la)
what, *quoi* (kwah)
when, *quand* (kahn)
where, *où est* (ooh-eh)
how much, *c'est combien* (say comb bee *ehn*)
credit cards, *les cartes de crédit* (lay kart duh creh *dee*)

If you're traveling to the French Riviera, check out our ***Nice and the French Riviera Made Easy*** guide (available in paperback and ebook). A few of the destinations featured in this handy guide are:

- Nice
- Villefranche-sur-Mer
- Monaco
- St-Tropez
- Cannes
- Antibes

Available at
www.madeeasytravelguides.com
www.amazon.com

Provençal Food & Drink Specialties
aïoli/ailloli, garlic mayonnaise
anchoïade, anchovy spread
banon, cheese dipped in *eau-de-vie* and wrapped in chestnut leaves
boeuf à la gordienne, braised beef dish
cachat, fresh cheese
cavaillon, a fragrant melon from the town of the same name. It looks like a small cantaloupe
champignon de pin, pine mushroom (a wild mushroom)
daube provençal, gravy with capers, garlic, and anchovies
escabèche, raw fish marinated in lime juice and herbs/a cold marinated sardine dish
estouffados, almond butter cookies
farigoule or **frigolet**, wild thyme
fromage fort, extremely soft cheese mixed with herbs, salt, pepper, and *marc*
herbes de Provence, mixture of herbs that includes fennel, lavender, marjoram, bay leaf, sage, rosemary, and thyme
lapin en paquets, rabbit pieces in a packet of bacon
lavande, lavender. Lavender blossoms are added to dishes such as *sorbet de lavande* (lavender sorbet)
lou maïs, corn-meal cake
marc, a strong liqueur made from distilling the residue of grapes (similar to Italian grappa)
muge, mullet
parme, amberjack (a fish)
pastis, anise-flavored aperitif. This is a Provençal word meaning mixture. It's a summer drink. Common brands are Pastis 51, Pernod, Ricard, Granier, Prado, and Henri Bardouin
petits farcis provençaux, stuffed vegetables
picodon, goat's-milk cheese
pissaladière, pizza-like tart with onions, black olives, and purée of anchovies and sardines
provençale, à la, with garlic, onions, herbs, and tomatoes ("Provence style")
quartiers d'orange glacés, caramelized orange sections
tapenade, mixture of black olives, olive oil, lemon juice, capers, and anchovies (a spread)

tian de Saint-Jacques et légumes provençal, sea scallops on a bed of chopped vegetables

tomates à la provençal, baked tomatoes stuffed with bread crumbs, garlic, and parsley

trouchia, an omelet (in most of France, this means trout)

violet de Provence, braid of garlic

Nice/French Riviera Food & Drink Specialties

bohémienne, eggplant and tomato casserole

daube à la niçoise, beef or lamb stew with red wine, tomatoes, and onions

farci, a dish of stuffed vegetables

lou pevre, goat's-milk cheese with coarsely ground pepper

lou piech, stuffed veal dish

niçoise, usually means with tomatoes, anchovies, vinegar, and black olives

pan bagnat, large round sandwich filled with olive oil, onions, olives, tomatoes, anchovies, and a hard-boiled egg. A specialty on the Côte d'Azur (means "wet bread"). This is a *salade niçoise* sandwich

pissaladière, pizza-like tart with onions, black olives, and purée of anchovies and sardines

ratatouille, eggplant casserole

salade niçoise, salad usually with tomatoes, anchovies or tuna, potatoes, vinegar, and black olives

socca, *crêpe* made with chickpea flour

stockfish, spicy fish stew

You'll also find such Italian pasta favorites as gnocchi and ravioli on many menus.

10. INDEX

Made Easy Travel Guides
Dining Guides
Menu Translators and Restaurant Guides

- *Eating & Drinking in Paris*
- *Eating & Drinking in Italy*
- *Eating & Drinking in Spain and Portugal*
- *Eating & Drinking in Latin America*
- *Eating & Drinking in Germany*
- *Wining & Dining in Paris*
- *Wining & Dining in Italy*

Travel Guides

- *Amsterdam Made Easy*
- *Barcelona Made Easy*
- *Berlin Made Easy*
- *Europe Made Easy*
- *Nice and the French Riviera Made Easy*
- *Italy Made Easy*
- *Madrid Made Easy*
- *Oslo Made Easy*
- *Paris Made Easy*
- *Paris Walks*
- *The Next Time I See Paris*
- *Provence Made Easy*
- *San Diego Made Easy*
- *Palm Springs Made Easy*
- *The Amazing California Desert*
- *Southern California Made Easy*

For a list of all our travel guides, and to purchase our books, visit
www.madeeasytravelguides.com

Printed in Great Britain
by Amazon

38238425R00068